GOD ONLY KNOWS

KNOWS

A CLASSIC ROCK ALBUM
INTERSECTS WITH
Christian Theology
& Living

To Don & Sherry:

TERRY AYCOCK

*Romans
12:1-2*

Terry Aycock

ISBN 978-1-68197-751-5 (Paperback)
ISBN 978-1-68197-752-2 (Digital)

Christian Faith Publishing, Inc.
296 Chestnut Street
Meadville, PA 16335
www.christianfaithpublishing.com

Printed in the United States of America

DEDICATION

Dedicated to my loving wife, Kay, who has been so steadfast in her love and strength;

To my daughters, Jennifer and Lauren, who are wonderful daughters and have been great encouragements and who are Beach Boys fans themselves;

And to my lifelong friend, David, who encouraged me to finish the book and who then made it possible to happen. Could not have done it without him!

DISCLAIMER

The inspiration for this book came from reflection on Brian Wilson's and The Beach Boys album *Pet Sounds* and how the titles of the songs and some of the words tended to lend themselves to such reflection on the Christian faith.

However, the contents and message of the book are in no way meant to imply a reflection of Brian Wilson's own beliefs, or are they endorsed by him or any of the members of The Beach Boys. While I would hope that would be the case, I want to be clear that no such implication is intended, or is any endorsement meant to be implied by the use of the name of the album and the songs that make up the content of the album.

The album stands alone as one of the greatest albums of pop and rock music. The contents of the book are not intended to be an interpretation of the lyrics of the songs but rather a reflection on both the titles and some of the words used in the songs.

CONTENTS

PREFACE

In the mid 1960's, I can recall seeing my older sister's collection of record albums. The one she always kept at the front of the rack was "Pet Sounds." She had the record player in her room, so she would occasionally invite me in and we would listen to the smooth harmonies of the Beach Boys. I can still sing the lyrics to most of the songs.

Terry Aycock has devised a creative way to merge the Beach Boy's songs with Christian theology and practice. The thirteen chapters are based on the song titles on the album. In this book the author deals with topics that range from original sin to the different views of eschatology. Sample chapters address the topics of doubt, God's Will, the character of God, the human dilemma, rest and leisure, prayer and the meaning of love.

The author refrains from using deep theological terms, so this book can be understood and appreciated by any reader. For readers interested in a deeper look, he has included an addendum on systematic theology defining each area in simple terms.

I believe you will be blessed as you enjoy each track of *God Only Knows: A Classic Rock Album Intersects Christian Theology and Living.*

Pastor David O. Dykes
Green Acres Baptist Church
Tyler, Texas

INTRODUCTION

I have an unfair advantage in understanding the words of this book. I grew up in the same small town, with the author, and some of the times he talks about sitting on a car and staring up into the heavens, and wondering about God, I was there because we were close childhood friends. In a small town there is not a lot to do, and sometimes that can be a blessing!

I can say this about the man who wrote this wonderful work—he became a Christian as a young man, even before High School, long before I did. There is no doubt in my mind that from a human viewpoint, my own salvation had a lot to do with Terry's consistent testimony through those young years, and into High School when many friends went to church every Sunday morning (for we were in the Bible belt) but I knew what they did on Saturday night! This gave me a mixed message and made it easy to stay away from church. However, I had two friends who were real, and I knew it, and Terry was one of them. I will always be thankful that his life was a clear testimony for Christ even from his youth, and all the way to the present.

I had the privilege of reading some of the first pages of this book when it was barely more than a thought being conceived in my friend's head. When Terry said, "I have an idea, I'm thinking about writing a book using the Beach Boys and their work to teach Biblical concepts," my first thought was, "Could you use Grand

Funk Railroad?" I did not like the idea. But when I read those first few chapters, I could not believe how well the stories took complex Biblical concepts and made them simple enough (and interesting enough) to cause the brand new Christian to give the book a read, and then accidentally understand the deep truths within. At the same time, a man like myself, who had been in the ministry for over thirty years, and learned so many of the "boxes" men could put God in, would also find the book not only inspiring, but thought provoking!

Terry has a unique gift of being able to talk about how theology can sometimes get in the way of knowing God, while at the same time stealthily teaching theology to the new and experienced student alike! Terry is many things to me, personally—a childhood companion; a life-time friend who can still make me laugh quicker and longer than anyone; a man who has gone through enough tribulation in life, while sticking with God, to be qualified to succor others and to talk about faith without hypocrisy; and above all things—a great story teller. Enjoy this book, and then pass it on to five other people, for to give is greater than to receive, and what a great gift this book would be.

David Mitchell, Pastor
Park Meadows Church
Corsicana, Texas
CEO and President
TradeWay Inc.
CEO
Exos Aerospace Inc.

PET SOUNDS THEOLOGY: BASIC CHRISTIAN THEOLOGY AND LIVING

Anyone growing up in the turbulent sixties who listened to AM radio is, at least, vaguely familiar with the music of The Beach Boys. Not everyone took to their music, favoring the more hip group from England, The Beatles, or others from the well known "British Invasion." But from the first moment I heard the harmonious sounds of The Beach Boys, I took to their music like a thirsty man takes to water. I drank it in day after day.

Respected by his musical peers but little known other than as a member of the group, their musical leader, Brian Wilson, was honing his craft. While there were and are Christians who bemoan the hedonism of many of the songs (Girls on the Beach, California Girls, Surfer Girl, The Little Girl I Once Knew, Help Me Rhonda, I Get Around, etc.), it was the complexity of the harmonies and the chord progressions as well as the compositions and arrangements of the songs that really began to catch the attention of musicians. I have heard musicians discuss his music and say that when you first hear Brian's songs, you think, *Yeah, I want to sing along with that.* Then they say that once you start trying to break down the music, the harmonies are extremely complex. Brian was among the first to be given artistic freedom to produce his own songs, and progression was meteoric. In a relatively short period, he progressed from the basic simplistic production of "Surfin" to the extremely complex "pocket symphony" we know as "Good Vibrations."

In the midst of this progression, he, along with lyricist Tony Asher, put together, in 1966, an altogether different type of album than the Beach Boys had ever done. It was christened as *Pet Sounds*. Given credit for changing the face of rock music, it was and is revered by those in the music industry and gave us lush melodies, beautiful harmonies, orchestral majesty, and a creativity not yet seen in the world of rock music. The counter bass lines were unheard of up to that time, as he was putting notes together to create harmonies that were unheard of in the rock music world.

Over time, I have listened to the album countless times and have absorbed the music as only one can do with such music.

Along the way, I became a Christian, a follower of Jesus Christ, and for a time, believed that I should "put away childish things," which included *Pet Sounds*. Unlike Andrew Oldham, who said he went from agnosticism to having faith because of listening to *Pet Sounds*, at this part of my journey, I threw away every Beach Boy album or tape I owned, including *Pet Sounds*. (In an interesting twist, I kept all of my singles, so there was some obvious conflicting struggle going on!) I felt I had crossed a line between enjoying the art and worshipping the artist, and the only thing I knew to do in obedience to the Lord was to get rid of the music of the artist. So I did.

In time, however, I began to understand better how music can be enjoyed for enjoyments sake, and *Pet Sounds* once again became a big part of my repertoire. The more I listened, the more I began to form in my mind the contours of an outline of a basic Christian primer, based on the titles and some of the words of the songs contained in the *Pet Sounds* album. It is a very emotional album, but the feelings it expresses are not only emotional but are those things we all think about and ponder in our minds as well.

All of us deal with reality and what is real, how we know that we know (or don't know), truth, sin, love, doubt, and faith. Yes, faith. Even those who do not claim Christ as Savior and Lord have faith in something or someone. So to these ends, I have written something that is basic and, I hope, helpful. I am not a theologian, philosopher, psychologist, sociologist, or even a scholar, but I have lived, studied, read, thought, and lived (did I say that already?). I have had good relationships, had broken relationships, and have pondered so much of this life that I simply wanted to write this in hopes of communicating to the fellow struggler.

Brian once said that in the making of the album, he and his brother, Carl, prayed often for guidance. They had grown up attending church and sang in the church choir, so there was at least that background. I have no idea what Brian actually believes or what Carl believed, so when he says they "prayed," I take that at face value. He has always said that making music is a spiritual thing for him and, a few years ago, wrote a short gospel-driven song entitled "Walking Down the Path of Life," in which he pleas, "Touch me, heal me, wash my sins away." There is only One who can wash our sins away, the person of Jesus Christ. So my hope is that Brian believes in the only One who hears our prayers. I don't know, but what I do know is that the music of *Pet Sounds* is in many ways blessed, and we are blessed to have it to enjoy. My hope is that we will be singing "That Same Song" when we stand before God.

In the meantime, if you have never listened to the music of *Pet Sounds*, do yourself a favor and buy it, download it, whatever you have to do, and listen to it and enjoy the journey. One's musical journey, as Paul McCartney once said, is not complete without listening to the album. It is a wonderful journey.

CHAPTER 1

Wouldn't It Be Nice?

"Wouldn't it be nice if we could wake up, in the morning, when the world is new?"
—Brian Wilson/Tony Asher

"I remember thinking the world would never be the same because of what born-again Christians would achieve in my lifetime. I remember actually thinking I was going to be exempt from responsibilities in the real world, since we would always have our own world where the wind would always be warm and the leaves would always be green."
—John Fischer

"Everything's supposed to be different than what it is here."
—Simon, *Grand Canyon.*

"Everybody's normal, 'til you get to know them."
—John Ortberg

Who among us hasn't fantasized about our lives? What we would do differently, what our childhood dreams and fantasies were, what we would do if we just had the time or money, or both. We are told to dream when we are young, and those dreams are often fantasies we imagine can be real.

But the truth is that we live in a real world in which dreams and fantasies are shattered every day. And people are disappointed every day because the reality they created in their heads is not even remotely connected to the reality that exists in our world.

My dream as a kid was to be the next Mickey Mantle. I wore number 7 on my baseball jerseys and watched every Saturday when the Yankees played, listening to the colorful play-by-play of Dizzy Dean and Pee Wee Reese (with names such as Dizzy and Pee Wee, colorful was a foregone conclusion!). I soared with the home runs and ached with the strike outs as if it was me up there at bat. But the reality is that I never became the next Mickey Mantle, or even a great high school or college player. I quit playing after eight years of baseball because I took up tennis and liked it better. I didn't have ground balls coming at me with the speed of light, bigger guys running over me as I covered the base, or baseballs being thrown at my head by out of control pitchers on the opposing teams. So much for dreams of grandeur.

One of the great challenges of Christian living is determining what real spirituality is and what fantasy is. With all due respect to Walt Disney and Brian Wilson, fantasy is not reality. We have all probably had the sentiment, "Wouldn't it be nice?" at some points along our existence. I know I certainly have. I have a friend of mine who fantasizes about pastoring in the mountains, not too far from a ski resort and ministering to the community there. "Wouldn't it be nice?" he says, and I would have to admit, it has a certain amount of appeal. And as fantasies go, his is not beyond the realm of reality.

But not all of us are in that state. Our fantasies can sometimes be scary or impossible for one reason or another. So what is real spirituality and what is fantasy? And what grounds us in reality when there is so much around us in our world that screams for the escape of fantasy, that cries for the escape of nihilism? Only a cursory look at the news, the movies, and the music we are bombarded with each day could lead one to an escape from it all, an escape into a fantasy world that avoids reality, that avoids responsibility, that seeks to run from a world that is "not the way it is supposed to be."

Karl Menninger was a psychiatrist who once wrote "Whatever Happened To Sin?" after years in practice. He stated that 75 percent of his patients could be cured if they would just admit to having sinned and then accepting forgiveness, but most would not, so they stayed in a terrible state of mind. In dealing with the distinction between reality and fantasy, this is a good place to start. Kind of like Julie Andrews in *The Sound of Music*, "Let's start at the very beginning. A very good place to start." So the "do-re-mi" for us will be starting by looking how we got this way to begin with. Without this basic understanding, reality becomes more difficult to grasp.

THE REALITY OF SIN

GK Chesterton is credited with saying that "the doctrine of original sin is the only experientially verifiable doctrine of the Christian faith." Many of the early church fathers, especially Augustine, were proponents of the doctrine of original sin. In 2008, Professor Alan Jacobs wrote the book *Original Sin: A Cultural History* and appeals to those with little or no interest in theology by using literary and historical references to bring some understanding to the doctrine. As one reviewer says, Jacobs aims to show that "it is not simply a description of a quaint story about a garden with an apple. It's an expression of what's wrong with all of us, an attempt to answer the question, *Whence all this evil?"* (Christianity Today, Jason Byassee, 7/08/2008).

Seventeenth century preacher and pastor, John Owens, dealt extensively with the teaching of "indwelling sin and temptation" and said that "the man that understands the evil of his own heart, how vile it is, is the only useful, fruitful, and solidly believing and obedient person." (Owens, pg. xviii) He begins his essays by stating, "The doctrine of indwelling sin stands out as one of the fundamental truths of our Christian faith" (Owens, pg. 3).

One of my favorite poems was penned by Edward Sill during the nineteenth century. It is entitled "A Fool's Prayer." The court jester in the poem is mockingly asked by the king to "make for us a prayer!" What follows is a prayer of great humility which has the following lines:

> No pity, Lord, could change the heart
> From red with wrong to white as wool;
> The rod must heal the sin: but, Lord,
> Be merciful to me, a fool!

The court jester had a great understanding of two major components of the Christian faith: sin and God's mercy. If we are to understand reality and how we got the way we are, we could learn from the court jester. There is something to this truth of original sin.

Several years ago, Cornelius Plantinga Jr., wrote what was voted by Christianity Today as its "Book of the Year" in 1996. It was entitled "Not The Way It's Supposed To Be: A Breviary of Sin." It should be required reading for at least those of the Christian faith who have an interest in sin (said fully with tongue-in-cheek) and our understanding of it today.

In his preface, he writes, "The awareness of sin used to be our shadow. Christians hated sin, feared it, fled from it, grieved over it...."

But the shadow has dimmed. Nowadays, the accusation *you have sinned* is said with a grin, and a tone that signals an inside joke" (Plantinga, pg. ix). He goes on to say that "self-deception about our sin is a narcotic, a tranquilizing and disorienting suppression of our spiritual central nervous system. *What's devastating about it is that when we lack an ear for wrong notes in our lives, we cannot play right ones or even recognize them in the performances of other*" (Plantinga, pg. xiii, emphasis mine).

Plantinga states his case much more eloquently and with a powerful grasp of literary usage of words. Mine is much simpler. We have been duped and have bought into it. We have, in a paraphrase of an immortal comic strip, met the enemy, and it is not us!

To be fair, not all Christians have agreed on the doctrine of "original sin." Jacobs quotes Charles Finney, one of the great evangelists of the nineteenth century, as calling the doctrine "subversive of the gospel, and repulsive to the human intelligence" (Jacobs, ix, *Original Sin*). Others, he goes on to say, have called the doctrine "repulsive" and "revolting," and still, others see it as an insult to the grace and loving-kindness of God. Blaise Pascal, on the other hand, "believed that without this particular belief we lack any possibility of understanding ourselves" (Jacobs, pg. x, *Original Sin*).

The doctrine of original sin has its foundation in the book of Genesis in the Old Testament. It is known more clearly as the "Fall of Man" (or mankind). Genesis 3 tells the story of what happened, how sin entered the world, and what was affected by this entrance, and what would be the consequences henceforth. We tend to think that only one or two things were affected (especially if you are a woman and have given birth to children!), but Romans 8:19–22 tells us that all of creation "was subjected to futility," and that it "will be set free from its slavery to corruption into the freedom of the glory of the children of God." Romans 5:12 makes it clear that "through one man sin entered into the world, and death through sin, and so death spread to all men, because all sinned."

Sin entered into our reality when Adam and Eve chose to disobey God and instead believe the lies of the serpent (the devil in master disguise). Many, even in the church today, do not believe this truth and think it makes for a nice story to tell children in Sunday school lessons, but that it is not real or truthful, but a good fairy tale. But Francis Schaeffer stated it this way: "Though some men do not like the teaching, the Bible continues like a sledge hammer, driving home the fact that evil has entered into the world of man, all men are sinners, all men now sin. Listen to God's declaration concerning the human race in Jeremiah 17:9: 'The heart is deceitful above all things, and desperately wicked; who can know it?'" (Schaeffer, *Genesis In Space and Time*, pg. 87) Romans 3:23 says, "All have sinned and come short of God's glory."

The road to reality, the road to recovery, in a manner of speaking, begins here. And this truth is not used to beat someone over the head, but it is used to help in understanding that only in starting here is true reality available. And true freedom. By seeing this as our starting point, it will free us to understand much else about ourselves, why we do some of the things we do, and how this truth helps to keep us out of fantasyland.

THE WORLD OF FANTASY

On pretty much a daily basis, we are informed through many forms of media, but especially *Oprah* and her current reruns, now that she has "retired" (and the fact that I don't have to spell out *The Oprah Winfrey Show* should speak volumes), that all of us are basically good, and that there are many paths to God. In fact, upon her retiring from her show, the show was pretty much a sermon from Oprah, along the lines of exactly what is referred to here. G-O-D is referred to as "the ultimate consciousness, the source, the force (and may the force be with you), the all of everything there is" (Terry Mattingly, Scripps Howard News Service, *Tyler Morning News*, June 4, 2011). Let's deal here with only this first concept, then deal with the second one later in the book.

I don't believe Oprah has done any cornering of any market on this fantasy. In sociology classes I attended in the 1970s, it was generally taught and generally accepted that all people are just really good people at heart, but society has somehow turned some people into bad people, and they are not to be held responsible for their actions, for it is, after all, society's fault (whoever this vague "society" is deemed to be).

Rebecca Manley, in her excellent book *Hope Has Its Reasons* shares the following story, which further illustrates this fantasy.

> A friend came over the other day very enthusiastic about a New Age seminar she had attended. She said, "I've finally realized there is no bad in me. I can only do good because I am good. God is in everything. Therefore I am God and God is me. I must only think positive thoughts and not let anything negative get in me or get me down. I don't say anything is wrong anymore, I just say, "It doesn't work for me."
>
> "You are the mother of teenagers," I responded. "How does your philosophy work out in raising children? Are they permitted to follow the same logic when you tell them to be in at midnight?" "Sorry, Mom, that just doesn't work for me." (Manley, *Hope Has Its Reasons*, pg. 55)

When I was a kid growing up in the sprawling little community of Mexia, Texas, I discovered early on in my own life the reality of "original sin." One of the great past times of my youth was collecting baseball cards. At one time, I had over 6500 cards (including some of the football cards I had collected, but baseball was dominant by far). I was a New York Yankee fan because I was a Mickey Mantle fan. So die-hard was I then that I am still a Yankee fan to this day. Baseball cards came in nickel packs. (I just wish I still had all of the cards today!) They always said we were buying the bubble gum in the packs, but most of the time, the gum was brick hard or just plain nasty! And we weren't totally stupid; we were hoping to get the latest Mantle card or anything Yankee at that time. We could care less about the gum.

In order to have money to purchase these cards, you either had an allowance or you contrived other ways to secure the needed funds to support this habit. My allowance (a quarter a week at the time) didn't go very far (five packs a week also meant no money for anything else, including the movie theater which was a quarter per movie). So I began to study ways to come up with other funds. "Study" would be stretching it a bit actually. It didn't take much study for this sinful little mind to conjure up a plan.

Every day, before Mom would head off to work, she had a routine. I began to realize that at a certain time every day, she would go into the bathroom to get ready, and she consistently took a certain amount of time. The bathroom was, of course, off limits and the door was closed, so I pretty much had the run of the rest of the house. Enter "original sin" (or at least, its carrier). I figured out a strategy that would place my hand into her purse and locate a quarter and maybe a dime to boot. So I began to steal money from Mom's purse to support my baseball card habit. I made sure I never took too much to make her suspicious (for example, if she had only one quarter that day, I did not take it but waited until the next day when more change would be available) and was never anywhere near her purse when she finished getting ready. Very nonchalant was I in fact.

No one taught me how to do that. No one showed me the ropes. No, I figured that one out all by myself because my little heart was full of deceit and evil intent. Some may think that wasn't a big deal, but ask a drug addict or an alcoholic or a thief how they got started. It was the first snort or drag, the first drink, the first theft. Proverbs reminds us that it is the "little foxes that spoil the vines." So called big things get their start with little things. And they all start because we are *not* basically good, but basically sinful, even though we do not like to hear it.

By itself, my story of stealing money out of my mom's purse does not prove the doctrine of original sin. However, it points to the truth that children must be taught to be truthful and moral and ethical but need no help at all to learn how to lie, be immoral, and unethical. Why, we should ask, is this the case? *Whence all this evil?* "*All* have sinned and fallen short of the glory of God" (Rom. 3:23) And this sin has its roots at the very beginning and through all of time. This is reality. This is not fantasy.

Sin, once in motion, tends to pick up steam. We have a tendency to think that one little white lie or one little misdeed is not much, but what happens as we practice sinful behavior is that we become more immune to its effects, and the behavior escalates until the conscience that we are all born with becomes numb. If this sounds like I am speaking from personal knowledge, it is because I am. I have seen how sin in my life can progress to such a point that I no longer even let it bother me and tend to shut out the Holy Spirit trying to nudge or kick me back into awareness.

I can illustrate this in two ways. First, when I moved to Oregon to attend seminary, I lived in a house with five other guys and had a small room with a window that faced directly across the street from the police station in the area. The garage doors of that station faced my window, and for the first couple of weeks, every time a police car was called into action, the sirens would blare as they came flying out of the underground garage. Not only was the noise from this loud, but half a block away, a main thoroughfare for eighteen wheelers stood with its majestic stoplight. Every time the light would turn red and one of these wheelers would have to come to a stop, the air brakes from the trucks would blare through the nighttime air. Needless to say, for the first two to three weeks, I slept very little with all of this noise finding its way through my window. A funny thing happened, however. I noticed that after a couple of weeks, I slept through the noise and did not even seem to notice it. I became almost immune to the noises even though they were still happening on a nightly basis. It occurred to me that this is exactly what happens when we continue to sin and never deal with it. We become immune to the "noise" and shut it out, so to speak. As a culture, we hear the gospel so much that we become immune to its message to the point that we don't really hear it anymore. It is a subconscious thing that happens without us even noticing what is happening, much the same way that I no longer was awakened by the noise out my window. The noise still happened, but my mind had just shut it out.

Secondly, the best show I have seen that illustrates this has been *Breaking Bad*. My wife and I got hooked on this show, and I told her that it was the best illustration I had ever seen of how sin progresses when left unchecked. One little lie became a bigger lie, which became a bigger lie until a mild-mannered chemistry teacher becomes a drug kingpin! The progression was amazing to watch, and though I don't know if that was the producer's intent, it certainly gave one of the best illustrations of such progression I have ever seen. Sin, left unchecked and unconfessed, will grow and grow just like a cancer that is left unchecked and not treated. And the reality is such sin will eventually take its toll and we carry or see the resulting effects in human carnage.

ALL DOGS GO TO HEAVEN?

Another fantasy we have come to adopt is that "all dogs go to heaven." It is a variation on the theme that all people will eventually be in heaven, regardless of who or what we have believed and how we have lived. "We are all striving for the same thing, and there are many roads to heaven." A loving God would not surely send any of His children to hell, or at least that is the way the fantasy is taught.

Recently, the Sunday morning version of the tabloids, which comes with our paper, *Parade Magazine*, had an interview with Angelina Jolie. Her mother was a strong Catholic and had Angelina in church on a regular basis, according to what the interview with Angelina said. Her partner, Brad Pitt, was raised in the Midwest and grew up in a family who worshipped in a local Baptist church. She was very affirming and affectionate in her speaking of her mother and her church background. And her humanitarian efforts and the money she and Brad have donated to victims in not only other countries, but their work with Katrina victims, should be applauded and admired.

What struck me about the interview, however, was the comment she made about the raising of their children and how they have a Bible, the Koran, Book of Mormon, the Torah, Hindu, and Buddhist teachings all available for their children so that their children can "choose." She said they want their children to pick their own religion instead of her or Brad "forcing" any belief on them.

On the surface, this sounds very noble, but children will eventually grow up and choose anyway, so why not give them some basis of truth as a start? We are led to believe that there is no absolute truth and there are many paths to God. "All dogs go to heaven," so to speak. Allan Bloom, in his 1986 publication *The Closing of the American Mind* had this to say: "There is one thing a professor can be absolutely certain of: almost every student entering the university believes, or says he believes, that truth is relative....The danger they have been taught to fear from absolutism is not error but intolerance. Relativism is necessary to openness; and this is the virtue, the only virtue, which all primary education for more than fifty years has dedicated itself to inculcating. Openness--and the relativism that makes it the only plausible stance in the face of various claims to truth and various ways of life and kinds of human beings--is the great insight of our times. The true believer is the real danger" (Bloom, *The Closing of the American Mind*, pg. 25–26).

In his book *The Reason for God*, Timothy Keller states the following when dealing with the question of how a loving God could send people to hell: "Our culture has no problem with a God of love who supports us no matter how we live. It does, however, object strongly to the idea of a God who punishes people for their sincerely held beliefs, even if they are mistaken" (Keller, *The Reason For God*, pg. 72). He goes on to clarify later in this chapter that, according to Romans 1:24, "All God does in the end with people is give them what they most want, including freedom from Himself" (Keller, pg. 82).

The twentieth century was one of the bloodiest centuries in human history. Two world wars, two atomic bombs, and countless other wars and internal skirmishes and civil wars have left millions dead and others marred for life. The Holocaust was one of the most gruesome periods in all of human history, and man's inhumanity toward man expressed in this horror has been amazingly and horribly duplicated in other places since then such as the Sudan, Darfur, the Congo, Rwanda, and parts of the Middle East as well as other places around the globe. For a century that was supposed to be one of educational enlightenment, more blood was spilled in that century than in all other centuries combined. So we must ask, if man is basically good, how are such atrocities explained? How does one who is basically "good at heart" treat fellow humans as experiments or cattle or laboratory rats? Again, *whence all this evil?* And can we honestly say with any amount of conviction at all that we really believe that the Hitlers, the Stalins, the Husseins, and the other sociopaths and psychopaths who have murdered and tortured and maimed count-less victims, can we really say that apart from God's grace imparted through faith in Christ and His finished work on the cross, such "dogs" are going to heaven and we want our mansions right next to theirs!? To "wake up" next door to them and say, "Howdy, neighbor?" Isaiah said it well: *"Come, let us reason together."*

Jesus said very clearly and without a bigoted, relativistic bone in his body: "I am the way, the truth, and the life. NO ONE comes to the Father except through ME" (John 14:6). All dogs, so to speak, will not—contrary to popular belief and desire—go to heaven.

Lost: Salvation Gained through Grace

The third fantasy comes from within the world of theology and the church. Throughout the history of Christendom, there has been an ongoing conflict which came into clearer focus during the time of the Reformation between what is known as Arminian and Calvinist views, and this has produced for us yet another fantasy. That is, that one who is saved by the grace of God can lose that sal-vation. To label this as a fantasy will probably cause more concern for some than the first two fantasies I mentioned, and that is a fact. As Abraham Lincoln said as he struggled with issuing the Emancipation Proclamation, "The subject is difficult and good men do not agree." This chapter and this book will not solve the centuries old debate, or even make such an attempt. Both sides quote biblical passages to support their theologies. This is not a full-blown critique of either Arminian teachings or of Calvin's theology. Personally, I don't think either of them were totally correct, and the church has wasted a lot of energy taking sides in this debate and throwing stones (in some cases during the time of the Reformation, quite literally!)

But here is the reason I place the "lost salvation" teaching in the realm of fantasy. Jesus used the "born again" language with Nicodemus for a purpose. And similar language to describe salvation is used elsewhere in the New Testament. As Jesus would often use terms that people would understand (look at all of his agricultural, farming, fishing, and cultural examples), his use of "born again" is significant.

Jonathan Edwards—the late great eighteenth century preacher, pastor, and philosopher—wrote a rather long treatise entitled *The Religious Affections* in which he addresses the very issue of what constituted a true salvation. It would be worth the time one should take to read his teaching, but the essence was that some so called conversions are "false conversions." Understand, Edwards wrote this on the heels of two "Great Awakenings" and had firsthand knowledge of "conversions" that turned out to not be conversions at all. They have all of the appearances of what a conversion should look like, but are, in actuality, false conversions. Just as there have been false pregnancies (all of the symptoms, all of the signs, but no baby in the uterus), there can be such experiences in the church. All of the symptoms, all of the initial outward signs, but no real change of heart, no real baby in the uterus, so to speak. On the other hand, there cannot be true conversions that do not result in a "second birth." One who is truly "born again" cannot be "unborn again."

LIVING IN COMMUNITY

While it is fine to write and talk about theological realities and fantasies, there is a deeper and harder reality to write about, and that is the gap that seems to exist between what we say we believe in the church and how we actually practice those beliefs. I am not referring to liturgy and worship but how we live these things among ourselves.

The title of the chapter often comes to mind when I think about this very dichotomy within the church.

After having been in the church for over sixty years and having been a Christian for over forty of those years, I am still struck by how we shoot our wounded rather than being the "hospital for the sick" that Jesus spoke of to the Pharisees. The reality is that we don't practice what we preach very well. "Wouldn't it be nice" if we would somehow learn to love one another rather than bicker over such minutia as we do?

While church discipline is probably the blind spot of our age on the one hand, on the other, we too readily want to play corrector and Holy Spirit for others and then leave the wounded to fend for him or herself. Is it any wonder that people leave the church and have no intention of coming back? I know there are other issues here, and that people use all sorts of excuses for leaving the church, but the reality is that we are ugly to one another so much of the time. We have this ugliness in the world. Why step into the church and just get more of the same?

I have spoken to businessmen and women who tell me that the businesses that advertise as "Christian-based businesses" are the ones that we should be certain to "stay away from." I worked briefly for a mortgage company that advertised as a "Christian-based mortgage company." What exactly is the difference between a mortgage done through a regular bank and a Christian-based mortgage company? Absolutely none. They go through the same process, the same regulations, the same type of closings at a title company. And I found that my brief experience at the first company was anything but Christian-based. And in fairness, I was no better than the one running the company. I went to my first closing, knowing that money was going to be exchanged outside of the closing, which is against regulations, but is done more often than you might believe. Neither the experience nor working there was an uplifting experience. And yet we wonder why people turn away from the church.

This is part of the reality of being a part of this organism we call the body of Christ. And it is pure fantasy to believe that, upon being saved, we escape this earthly body and all is just sunshine and roses from here on in. But the question is fair and must be asked, How do true born-again Christians take their faith and become so hateful and so prideful? At the risk of being "right," we lose our saltiness in the world because our rightness becomes hateful and downright ugly.

Several years ago, I was a worker at a Francis Schaeffer Seminar in Portland, Oregon. His seminar featured him and C. Everett Koop, the future surgeon general under Ronald Reagan, and was based on their book *Whatever Happened to the Human Race?* I was a bit unprepared for the stir the seminar would create, and upon arriving at the civic center, I was a bit surprised to find picketing going on outside of the center. On the one side were the prolifers and on the other were those who were calling themselves pro-choice.

During one of the breaks from selling books at the tables, I went outside to watch. I was kind of fascinated, as I had never actually seen picketing up close and personal, but had just seen it happening on television.

Two things struck me as I stood there. One was the ugliness I was watching from both sides as they spouted their slogans at one another. The other was the separate conversations that I heard and observed taking place as both handed out their pamphlets and the ugliness with which this was happening. A lady approached me and handed me a pamphlet advocating her pro-choice beliefs, and I struck up a dialogue with her. I discovered that she was the president of the group, but I also discovered she was pleasant and open to real, meaningful dialogue. We were having a genuinely good conversation stating our opposing views, until we were interrupted by a fairly rude prolifer who all but condemned this woman to hell on the spot, smugly convinced that he had witnessed for Jesus that day. As he left, she turned to me and said, "He is why I have so much trouble with the prolife position. You tend to be so self-righteous and smug and just mean-spirited." I apologized for his rudeness and told her that we were not all so ruthless and invited her in to the seminar. She wasn't changing my mind, nor was I going to change hers that day, but I wanted her to know that the same Jesus who died for me died for her and loved her just as much as He loved me. We actually ended up thanking one another for the conversation, and she said that this had at least given her hope that someone on the opposing side would at least have a dialogue about the issue.

I tell this story not to exalt anything I did that day (for I have certainly had my moments of ugliness) but to point out the ugliness that I saw exhibited from Christians that day. If we cannot exhibit love to all people, and especially to those of the faith, how can we expect the world to think that we live in anything other than a fantasyland that has nothing to do with real spiritual life? Wouldn't it be nice?

TYING IT ALL TOGETHER

We live in an age in which the term "spirituality" is thrown around and thrown out like candy at a Macy's parade. We hear people say that they are "spiritual" or that they are into "spirituality." People are "getting in touch" with their true "spiritual selves." They use references from everything to the Bible to Vedic teachings to the Koran to L. Ron Hubbard to New Age gurus such as Deepak Chopra, and on and on.

So why this chapter on fantasy and reality? Well, four things need to be established early on before moving forward.

First, we need to have a clear understanding that we are where we are because of sin. It is not some psychological, sociological, or chemical malfunction that has those of us on planet Earth where we are. As Dr. Menninger so eloquently stated, "Whatever happened to sin?" It is first and foremost in admitting we have a sin problem to deal with that sets us straight in our quest for reality.

Second, it needs to be made clear that Jesus wasn't being bigoted or narrow-minded when He made it clear that despite all of the fantasies that are thrown at us, He is the only way to heaven, the only way to salvation, the only way to the Heavenly Father. For all of the praise and adulation Jesus receives for being a great moral teacher and a great prophet by those who do not embrace Jesus as Savior and Lord, they miss the most important part of His teaching, and that He is clearly, from His own mouth, the only way to the Father, the only way to heaven. The Bible is clear that while God clearly desires all to be saved, the only way is through His Son, Jesus. How God works this out for those who have never heard of Jesus before they die is His to decide and certainly not for us. That does not negate the fact that Jesus clearly tells us the only way to the Heavenly Father.

Third, once you and I are in His arms of salvation, we are safe and secure for all of eternity. John says in 1 John 5:13, "These things I have written to you who believe in the name of the Son of God, in order that you may know that you have eternal life." The Greek term that is used for *know* is a term that means that we can "know beyond any doubt" that we can have an understanding that goes beyond mere head knowledge and know to the depths of our souls, from our head down to our shoes, so to speak, that we have eternal life. There is something wonderfully powerful about knowing that we are completely secure, and that nothing can separate us from the love of Christ once we are securely in His arms. He will never let go. This is the reality we can live in confidently.

Finally, we need to see that spiritual reality must have some teeth in it if it is to be effective and real. That means that the breech between fantasy and reality in the Christian community must be closed, and we must live what we say. Not ever perfectly, for no person can, but certainly consistently, lovingly and with an effort to put the virtual reality guns down and stop shooting our wounded. We all hurt at different times, we all fall at different times, we all need help at different times. Living in community means loving one another in the way that Christ loved us. We need to practice extending the same grace to others that Christ extended to us. *Wouldn't it be nice? Absolutely!*

CHAPTER 2

You Still Believe in Me

"The essential thing 'in heaven and earth' is... that there should be a long obedience in the same direction."

—Friedrich Nietzsche

"Why is life given to a man whose way is hidden, whom God has hedged in? For sighing comes to me instead of food; my groans pour out like water."

—Job 3:23–24

"What faith it takes to believe that one's life is noticed by God and that this is enough!"

—Kierkegaard

"We were meant to be inhabited by God and to live by a power beyond ourselves. Human problems cannot be solved by human means."

—Dallas Willard,
The Great Omission, pg. 17

The generation of instant coffee and instant tea has been so touched by this addiction to everything instant that perseverance in anything, let alone faith and/or belief, has become nearly obsolete. Yet there are reasons beyond the cultural influences that create questions and doubts and serious seasons of reflection on continuing to believe.

My wife's grandmother had a rather eloquent way of stating what we all experience but seldom express verbally. She once said to my wife's own mother, "In life, it's just one damn thing after another." This is certainly one way of looking at things, and if we are honest, we have all felt the frustration of having one thing upon another happen in our lives and wondering what in heaven and earth is going on.

The sentiment expressed in the second song on the *Pet Sounds* album is actually one that is being expressed from a young man to a young woman. "And after all I've done to you, so faithfully, you still believe in me." I have thought that in the community of faith, we sometimes think this way, in something of a twist on the words, about how we are thinking about God. Surely, we think, as we shake our fists toward God, He must marvel that we still believe in Him after all we have perceived He has done to us!

One of my all-time favorite movies is *Forrest Gump*. I have seen it at least fourteen times, and to both of my daughter's embarrassments and horrors, I have the voice Tom Hanks uses for Forrest down pat. And I am not afraid to use it! (I only hear "Amen's!" when I use the voice to say, "I'm not a smart man, but," and I am usually stopped right there!) There is one scene in the movie that illustrates what I have been saying regarding our doubts and personal fist shaking. Lt. Dan, the character played brilliantly by Gary Sinise, is sitting atop the mast of the shrimp boat in the midst of a massive storm in the ocean and is shaking his fist at God while screaming, "It's just You and me. C'mon, is this all You got?! C'mon!" He and Forrest make it through the storm, and later in the movie, Forrest informs his listeners that "I think Lt. Dan made his peace with God."(Only, he says it like "Gawd!") He had lost both legs in the Vietnam war and had spent years angry at God, and the scene during the storm was the climax of that anger.

Many of you reading this have had your own experiences that have led you to doubt, to be angry with God, to question your beliefs, to wonder if God is truly fair, to wonder if this God you have said you believed is really worth believing. I know I have certainly had my moments. But what Nietzsche said so brilliantly is worth repeating: "The Christian faith is a long obedience in the same direction." There is nothing "instant" about such an obedience.

THE DILEMMA OF DOUBT

When dealing with belief and what we believe and in whom we believe, the issue of doubt has been an issue the church has kept at bay for some time. If someone expressed doubt, he or she was almost shamed for having such thoughts. A true believer, we were told, just never had doubts about his or her faith. Doubting became akin to the "unpardonable sin," and doubters and doubting were shunned. We have been pointed to "doubting Thomas" in the Bible as an example of why we should never doubt or have any such thoughts.

That all sounds well and good, but the problem that persists is that, if we have had any thoughts about our faith at all that have gone beyond the depth of a thimble, we have had moments or periods of doubt. It has been expressed in the form of questions, such as, "Why did this happen to me?" or "Why did God allow this to happen?" or "This is not fair, and I want to know why it happened," or as Philip Yancey has expressed in his book *What Good Is God?* The problem we face, in believing, is that this dilemma of doubt that can raise its head at the most inopportune times and at times we are most vulnerable. And if we are to "still believe in Me," we must not only admit to such times of doubt, but also know how to deal with doubt in such a way that both allows for such times of doubting and keeps us from allowing such doubt to submarine our faith and in whom we believe.

One of my favorite albums is Elton John's *Blue Moves*. (Those of you reading this from a younger generation would be interested to know that an "album" is what my generation had before there were CDs, iPods, downloads, and all of the technology that I have to ask my daughters and grandsons to show me how to use!) One song on that album is titled "If There's a God in Heaven (What's He Waiting For?)." When dealing with doubt, it is a question that even the most devoted of Christians have asked. We watch parents slowly melt away with Alzheimer's and wonder. We watch as friends and families discover they are dying from cancer and wonder. We are touched by tragedy when we or a friend or loved one loses a son or daughter or spouse or parent in a tragic accident, and we wonder. We watch as children we have loved spiral downward in a world of drugs they got caught up in, and we wonder. We watch as our sons and daughters go off to war and become casualties of that war, and we wonder. And those who have been on the battlefield and in war zones and have fought the fight see the cruelties of war and see their buddies killed and friends maimed and then wonder. The dilemma of doubt becomes a companion that comes along beside us to try to get us to question God, and we ask, "What is He waiting for?" How do we continue to have faith and believe when the world is throwing so much at us in an attempt to get us to stop believing? How do we deal with this dilemma of doubt?

DEALING WITH OUR DOUBTS

One of the great blessings and curses of our time is that we have access to so much reading material that we should never be at a loss. And to make things even easier (at least for the technologically advanced, who actually understand all of the new technical devices), we have come up with the iPad, the Nook, and the Kindle. Now we can have a traveling library with us that is portable and accessible and lightweight!

If, however, one prefers an actual physical manifestation of the technical downloads (in past times, called a "book"), there are plenty of those available as well. Walk into any Barnes and Noble or Books-A-Million, and you are greeted with row upon row of reading literature. I absolutely love going into bookstores and rarely leave without a new book.

In the midst of these aisles of books, there are literally hundreds of self-help titles and more available under Psychology, Health and Diet, and Relationships. We have answers for metabolic problems, overeating, under eating, obesity, anxiety, exercising, walking, running, jogging, and how to deal with sexual malfunctions, including just what to do if your Viagra goes haywire! We have physical, relational, financial, and managerial gurus for just about any topic or subtopic that any of these would entail. You would think we just about have ourselves figured out by now.

When it comes to dealing with doubt, it seems we know we haven't a clue when it comes to having it all figured out. So what do we do when the doubt of which I have been speaking overruns our thought life and seems to entrap us into doubting all that we know is actually true? The Bible is a very good place to start.

I have often seen throughout my life that there is a very fine line between real faith and real stupidity, and the key is knowing where that line actually lies. We have probably all seen people do completely idiotic things, claim idiotic things, and then somehow manage to get "Jesus" tied into their lame-brained schemes. I may have been one of those you saw! There is a right way to be a "fool for Christ," but some of the things I have seen people do that get faith and Jesus mistakenly connected into the foolishness are not what

Paul meant when he said we are to be "fools for Christ." Hebrews
11:1–3 gives us a clear understanding of how faith is to be defined.

> Now faith is the assurance of things hoped for,
> the conviction of things not seen. For by it the
> men of old gained approval. By faith we under-
> stand that the worlds were prepared by the word
> of God, so that what is seen was not made out of
> things which are visible. (NASB)

Why am I saying anything about faith at this point? Weren't we
talking about doubt? Yes, and one of the antidotes to doubt is faith.
Christians are called upon to believe what we have not seen and to
believe Him whom we have not seen.

In the 1960s, the Beatles recorded a beautiful song entitled "Let
It Be." "When I find myself in times of trouble, mother Mary comes
to me. Speaking words of wisdom, let it be… And though the night
is weary, there is still a light that shines on me. Shine until tomorrow,
let it be." There is probably no greater struggle in life than when we
are dealing with doubt because of circumstances or events that have
happened that have brought our doubts to the surface and brought
us into a real place of darkness in our minds. I am not completely
sure what light Lennon and McCartney were speaking of, but the
light the Bible speaks of is the light of Scripture, the light of Jesus,
the light of the Holy Spirit. "And this is the message we have heard
from Him and announce to you, that God is light, and in Him there
is no darkness at all" (1 John 1:5, NASB).

Despite all of the attempts to neatly package answers to our
Christian walk, there is no magic how-to formula that sets us on a
path to dealing with our doubts. However, remembering faith and
how it is defined and learning to trust in that which we cannot and
have not ever seen is a good starting point.

The story is told that Albert Einstein was once visiting a class-room in which a professor friend of his had invited him to come and lecture. Before getting started, the professor told his class that he did not believe in God because you could not prove him. You could not see, smell, or touch this so-called God; therefore, He could not exist. He then introduced Dr. Einstein, who began by looking at the class and asking them, "Have any of you ever seen your professor's brain? Have you ever touched it? Have you ever smelled it?" When no one replied that they had, he pointedly said, "Then I suppose that proves that the professor's brain doesn't exist!"

The story of Joseph from the Old Testament is a story that illustrates just how one is to hold on to faith in very dark circumstances. We have kind of popularized the story with a Broadway production of "Joseph and the Technicolor Dreamcoat" (complete with none other than Donny Osmond at one time in the starring role), but the story is a powerful story on one who kept his perspective.

Joseph, if we recall, was the youngest of his brothers and the favored son of his father. Being a favored son cannot always be great place to be for the son. Some of you were either a "favored son" or the brother of one, and you remember how that felt. Such did Joseph's brothers feel for him, a raging jealousy that led them to eventually sell their brother to a band of men who then took him into Egypt where he eventually ended up in the prison of the Pharaoh. However, he correctly interpreted a dream for the Pharaoh, and he eventually became the second in command in all of Egypt, laying aside grain and food for the seven-year famine, which hit the region. His brothers, sent by a grieving father who did not know of Joseph's situation and thought him to be dead for years, came to him for food, not knowing or recognizing who he was. The story tells us he went into another room and wept when he recognized his brothers and then came back and quizzed them about their father and their situation. I am making a longer story short here, but he finally revealed himself to them and, in essence, said to them, "I am your brother Joseph, whom you sold into Egypt. But now do not be grieved or angry with yourselves, because you sold me here; for God sent me before you to preserve life." In other words, what the brothers intended for evil, God had other intentions and preserved a nation because of what transpired.

Joseph could very well have doubted God and why he had been sold, had been thrown into prison, and why he was in the circumstances in which he found himself. Being just as human as you or I, I suspect he may have had at least a moment or two when he doubted. He had every right, it would seem, to doubt God and to doubt his faith, but he chose not to do so. He chose to trust, to have faith, to believe in that which he had not seen. What a lesson for me, what a lesson for you in one aspect of how we can deal with doubt.

But it is never that easy, is it? Reading the story of Joseph, it almost seems easy, but it is foolish to think it was easy for Joseph. Ravi Zacharias, in his book *The Grand Weaver* writes of the death of his friend Robert Fraley, who died in the same plane crash that claimed the life of the famous golfer, Payne Stewart, as well. He spoke of Fraley's godly character and had this to say:

> One cannot but raise the question, as harsh as it sounds, Why do so many destructive people live to a ripe old age, while so many who dedicate themselves to serving others and God seem to get snuffed out so soon? Does anyone who observes life philosophically not at some stage ask this question?... The questions reveal the simplistic nature of our analyses and conclusions -- as if we know all there is to know." (Zacharias, *The Grand Weaver*, pg. 34)

As we further explore how we deal with doubt, we should remember that "every journey requires deliberate steps." And these steps require the recognition that what is involved in the process is our hearts. Not the physical organ, but that part of us that drives our being, that moves our emotions, that moves our souls. And as Zacharias so clearly points out "at the end of your life one of three things will happen to your heart: it will grow hard, it will be broken, or it will be tender. Nobody escapes" (Zacharias, *Grand Weaver*, pg. 40).

So to deal with doubt, we must return to our roots, first of all, and that is the faith or the trust we must have in God in dealing with our doubts.

Second, the Bible and scriptural stories and verses must remind us of who God is and who we are, in that order! We must have constant reminders that God truly is light and in Him is no darkness.

Finally, in the midst of our questions and in the midst of our doubts, we must continue to pray. I will deal more with this in chapter 4, but I need to say it here. I know, I know. When in the midst of doubt, it becomes extraordinarily difficult to pray, and if we are honest, we wonder if prayers from us at such times go much beyond the ceilings of our rooms. Remember, we are not alone, or are we "lone rangers." Christians live in a community of faith, so when doubts come (and if you are living and doing even a smattering of thinking, they will) get others to pray on your behalf.

YOU STILL BELIEVE IN ME

I began this chapter with a quote from philosopher Friedrich Nietzsche. Hebrews 12:1–2 must have been a part of the source of his sentiment. It reads:

> Therefore, since we have so great a cloud of witnesses surrounding us, let us also lay aside every

encumbrance, and the sin which so easily entangles us, and *let us run with endurance the race that is set before us,* fixing our eyes on Jesus, the author and perfecter (finisher) of faith, who for the joy set before Him endured the cross, despising the shame, and has sat down at the right hand of the throne of God.

Long-distance runners have told me that, at some point along the journey, a second and sometimes third and fourth winds kick in, and the running becomes a delight. Eric Liddell, Scottish Olympic runner in the 1920s and one of the central characters of the movie *Chariots of Fire*, tells his sister at one point in the movie that "God has made me fast, Jennie, and when I run, I feel His pleasure." I have never been much of a runner and have certainly never been fast, but the sentiment these runners express is something of what I hear the writer of Hebrews saying. As we run with endurance the race that is set before us, there will be obstacles, there will be doubts, there will be rainy days, there will be mud slung all over us, there will be stone bruises on our feet, and we may even develop turf toe on occasion, but as we fix our eyes where they are supposed to be, we will be given the gift of continuing to "still believe" in the "Me" who is the Lord God. Like Eric Liddell, we will "feel His pleasure."

CHAPTER 3

That's Not Me

"Hmmm. A room full of empty people."
—Line from Neil Simon play,
"Murder By Death"

"I yam what I yam, and that's all I yam."
—Popeye

"When you deal with human beings, you have come to the 'as is' corner of the universe… When we enter relationships with the illusion that people are normal, we resist the truth that they are not….One of the great marks of maturity is to accept the fact that everybody comes 'as is'."
—John Ortberg,
Everybody's Normal Till You Get To Know Them

"I had to prove that I could make it alone, now, but that's not me. I wanted to show how independent I'd grown now, but that's not me."
—Brian Wilson/Tony Asher

One of the great terms that our generation has adopted to explain everything that we either can't explain or that we think we know so much about is the term "dysfunctional." If we don't have perfect bodies, our bodies are dysfunctional. If we don't make perfect grades, our classes are dysfunctional. If we fail or fall in anything, it is because something was dysfunctional. If we don't have perfect families, especially if there has been divorce, we are labeled as dysfunctional families. Anything short of perfection gets labeled as being dysfunctional.

It only takes living past about thirty before one begins to wake up to the fact that everything about this life is dysfunctional in some form or fashion, even families who, to the naked eye, appear to have it all together. To take an oft quoted line borrowed from Shakespeare, "There is something rotten in the state of Denmark." Not all of us may live in Denmark, but we do get the full meaning of this comment. Something is not quite right with all of us, and this is not limited to those we have determined are psychopaths or sociopaths. All of us have screws loose somewhere in our psychological makeup.

When I attended college, I distinctly remember thinking that every psychology major who I met was in that major for a reason. They all seemed to be certifiable nut cases, or at least on the verges of being one. So above and beyond this in my own mind was I that I was extraordinarily resistant to learning anything in the first psychology class in which I enrolled. All of the Freudian, Skinnerian, and Jungian theories were obviously designed for those who were the nut cases and certainly had nothing to teach me. No, I was perfectly normal and none of the theorizing, and psychological mumbo-jumbo was in the least bit applicable to me. *Obstinate* is the operative word here.

It is often said that God must have a great sense of humor. I am certain He does, though that is not the central most important characteristic He possesses. However, as humor goes, He must draw great delight in watching His children get full of themselves as I did when it came to psychology. Years later, I married a psychology major. So much for the wacko-psycho thinking on my part. The heavens shake with laughter.

At this point, you may be asking what has any of this to do with the Christian faith and what is it doing in a book, which is supposed to be dealing with basic Christian beliefs. It is a fair question to ask, and were I many years younger, I would be asking the same thing. However, with age comes some amount of realization that all of us are "nut cases" to some extent, and that one of the effects of the fall was the effect it had on that part of our being which we would label the "psyche." We do things that we do not understand and look in the mirror and say, "That's not me." In short, we are all psychologically damaged in some way and in desperate need of understanding (a) that we are damaged, and (b) that we need help in repairing the damages.

PSYCHOLOGICAL PROBLEMS AND PEOPLE

Francis Schaeffer wrote of this issue in his book *True Spirituality*. He had this to say in regards to what has happened:

> Let us be clear about this. All men since the fall have had some psychological problems. It is utter nonsense, a romanticism that has nothing to do with biblical Christianity, to say that a Christian never has psychological problems. All men have psychological problems. They differ in degree and they differ in kind, but since the fall all men have more or less a problem psychologically. (Schaeffer, *True Spirituality*, pg. 132)

None of us fully knows our own selves, much less fully knows someone else. However, there are some things we can know just from sharing a common humanity, a common personhood. One of those is that we all struggle with issues of identity. We all struggle with those areas within our minds that bring us to the brink of really foolish and sometimes costly actions. Sometimes, these are even suicidal. But we have all been through or are going through trying to find out "who we are" and what makes us tick, so to speak.

Because of certain situations I have found myself in, and because of my rather curious nature anyway, I have been one of the privileged number of people who have taken a rather sizable amount of psychological tests. Everything from the Minnesota Multiphasic Personality Inventory (three times, mind you) to DISC (three times also) to Meyers-Briggs to multiple other tests. I asked one of the counselors administering one of the tests if the test makers had some kind of an anal or bowel movement fixation. I had never been asked so many times in so many different ways about my bathroom habits. I was actually rather amused by the end of the test and was tempted to give them really crazy answers just to see what the results would be! I was told that interpreters of the test can tell certain things about a person by how many bowel movements they have in a day and what kind of bowel movements, etc. I am amused by many things, and I have to admit that this made me laugh. "Ah, you're type A, sir, because you have x number of movements per day, and you like having control. (What do they do with illnesses or other food situations that cause, aah, loose movements? Control? Ha!) We are able to tell this by the number and kind of movements you have." Something about this just strikes me as odd and funny. Alas, the tests continue to ask such questions.

These tests are given, however, for very good reasons. Such tests do help us to discover things about ourselves and help us to get to the core of our psyche. But they are not the end all to be all. The results are not the final answer. While these tests may give us some indicators about who we are and how we respond and what we like or dislike, etc., they will never fully explain us, for we are full of complexities and inconsistencies and contradictions. In a nutshell (no pun intended here either!), we are psychologically dysfunctional from the beginning. While we can know things about ourselves clearly enough to say "That's not me," it is true that we all have problems psychologically.

TRANSFORMATION AND PSYCHO-CYBERNETICS

The Bible tells us many things about ourselves, not the least of which is that we are in desperate need of transformation. Isaiah 53:6 says, "All of us like sheep have gone astray, each of us has turned to his own way." Jeremiah 17:9 tells us, "The heart is more deceitful than all else and is desperately wicked; Who can understand it?" The Psalmist writes in Psalm 51:5–6, "Behold, I was brought forth in iniquity, and in sin my mother conceived me. Behold, Thou dost desire truth in the innermost being." He further says in Psalm 55:4–5, "My heart is in anguish within me. And the terrors of death have fallen upon me. Fear and trembling come upon me, and horror has overwhelmed me." Romans 3:23 tells us, "All have sinned and fall short of the glory of God." The litany of verses informing us of our condition goes on and on, but you get the picture. We are in desperate need of transformation, in desperate need of a change of heart, in desperate need of psychological repair. In short, we are in desperate need of salvation.

Other religions actually agree with Christianity on this point. In Hinduism, karma is at play and through recycling, one may actually reach nirvana at some point. In Buddhism, there is an Eightfold Path one must follow to be transformed. In the Muslim world, one must continually appease Allah. The point is that each religion, though at a fundamental and crucial difference with Christianity as to the solution, recognizes that something is fundamentally wrong with each of us, and in order to "right the ship," steps must be taken to change this.

The Bible calls this "transformation." When Jesus spoke to Nicodemus, He told him, "Truly, truly, I say to you, unless one is born again, he cannot see the kingdom of God" (John 3:3). When Paul wrote to the Romans, he urged them on by saying, "And do not be conformed to this world, but be *transformed* by the renewing of your mind, that you may prove what the will of God is, that which is good and acceptable and perfect." (Rom. 12:2) When he wrote to the church at Galatia, he said, "I have been crucified with Christ and it is no longer I who live, but Christ lives in me; and the life which I now live in the flesh I live by faith in the Son of God, who loved me, and delivered Himself up for me" (Gal. 2:20).

Years from now, when we are history and our history is being told, one of earmarks of our time that will be told is our obsession with plastic surgery. We spend millions of dollars each year getting nipped and tucked, stretched, lifted, lipo-sucked, lap-banned, and gastro bypassed. With our youth fading, we are willing to spend a fortune to try to restore such youth. All age groups trying to look like they are twenty-five again and doing all within their pocketbooks to make it happen. And some even adding cushion to their posteriors, doing what time will eventually take care of anyway!

In 1960, Dr. Maxwell Maltz published a dynamic book, which is still popular and sold today, entitled *Psycho-Cybernetics*. I read this book back in the early 1970s. Dr. Maltz was a plastic surgeon whose job it was to perform such surgeries on those seeking to take out wrinkles and literally transform their look. He began to notice that, even when such surgeries were extraordinarily successful and the people came away looking absolutely beautiful, people were still unhappy and thought they were ugly. This, in spite of what the mirror was telling them. They would look at themselves and say, "That's not me." Literally. Interestingly enough, his conclusion was that he could change the outer being, but what really needed changing was the inner being, the inner thought life. Thus, Psycho-Cybernetics. Jesus said it in this manner: "Hear, and understand. Not what enters into the mouth defiles the man, but what proceeds out of the mouth, this defiles the man" (Matt. 15:10–11). His solution? "Come to Me, all who are weary and heavy-laden, and I will give you rest" (Matt. 11:28). It is the inner person that is in need of transformation, and long before Dr. Maltz reached his conclusion, Jesus was telling us the importance of our inner person.

Because we are all damaged goods upon arrival, such a transformation of thought is absolutely necessary. Our psyches are a mess, and no amount of outer transformation will work until the inner person is transformed. We can nip and tuck all we want, but unless we nip and tuck what is inside, it is an exercise in futility. The transformation the Bible speaks of is one that takes place because our minds are being constantly renewed through studying of God's Word. *That* is real and lasting transformation.

PSYCHOLOGIES ANSWERS

Most of the boomer generation is at least somewhat familiar with Sigmund Freud and his powerful influence on psychological studies. How many times have we heard or said, "Oops, Freudian slip!" Meaning, we said what we meant because our subconscious spoke it, but we really didn't intend to say what we did! Lesser known to the boomers is B. F. Skinner, at least by name. His influence is just as powerful, however, as it was he who taught that we are determined by our environmental conditioning.

Another influential teaching, which we hear little about anymore, was linguistic analysis. This was popularized by the book *I'm*

OK - You're OK. A few years after this was published, a Christian author and psychologist published a response to this. His title was a thing of artistic beauty: *I'm Not OK, You're Not OK, But That's OK!* One has to enjoy such a classic response, and one that is more biblically accurate.

So we accurately ask such questions as, "Are we environmentally determined?" "Are we products of our subconscious?" "Are we determined by our ego, super-ego, and/or libido, and is everything about us set in motion by our sex drive and our sexual fantasies?" "Are we determined by nothing more than our genetic code, our DNA?" "Are we nothing more than a collision of atoms in the universe, which sets in motion our pre-determined course for life?" The questions posed from the different psychological views and studies are an endless stream of thought and dialogue.

While it is safe to say that studies in psychology have helped us understand some of who we are and why we do some of the things we do, the situation we have encountered in the church has been to "psychologize" so much of our behavior that we have pastors, teachers, and other leaders explaining behavior that is in actuality just plain sin, by explaining such behavior away. One well-known pastor even went so far as to say that the "loss of self-esteem" is what is actually "hell." That there is no such real place as hell, just a loss of self-esteem. I am sure that the rich man in the parable of the rich man and Lazarus (Luke 16: 19–31) would be relieved to know that what he was *actually* experiencing was just a loss of self-esteem, not the "agony in this flame" that he said he was experiencing!

Some of the studies done in the field of psychology have certainly come to help us understand the human mind and the reasons why we do some of the things we do. However, psychology does not and cannot explain sin, only behavior which they fail to call sin. And it is this sin which produces sinful behavior.

For example, recent examples of parents who have killed their children are informative for us here. Psychology may be able to explain some of the psychoses involved, but it cannot explain the "sin that so easily besets us." And to explain such behavior away is neither helpful nor accurate because then what gets blamed is not the person but the psychosis itself.

It would be helpful to hear what psychologist and professor of psychology, Dr. Paul Vitz, says in this regard. "Forgiveness and repentance are not part of any standard psychological theory. From Sigmund Freud to Carl Jung to Carl Rogers to cognitive and behavioral therapy, these concepts receive no emphasis. He goes on to say that "psychological problems, however real, often do not have psychological answers; they have moral, spiritual, and theological answers" (Dr. Paul Vitz, "Leaving Psychology Behind," essay in *No God But God*, editors Os Guinness and John Seel, pg. 109).

Again, the studies of psychology help us in unlocking and understanding some about the human condition, but such studies are scientific in nature and cannot be thus conclusive about the very nature of men and women. Again, quoting Dr. Vitz, "Psychology cannot heal our deepest hurts or answer our strongest yearnings, and it is certainly not a pool in which to gaze perpetually at our own reflection. *At its best*, psychology is a stepping stone – we should use it to move on" (Vitz, *No God But God*, pg. 110). Only a clear understanding of the biblical teaching of human nature provides us with the counterpart to the statement, "That's not me," and helps each of us to begin to get a grasp on who we are so that we can say conclusively and with assurance, "That *is* me." Hallelujah!

CHAPTER 4

Don't Talk (Put Your Head on My Shoulders)

"Don't talk, put your head on my shoulders. Don't talk, close your eyes and be still. Don't talk, and listen to my heart beat. Listen, listen, listen."
—Brian Wilson/Tony Asher

"In everything by prayer and supplication with thanksgiving let your requests be made known to God."
—Philippians 4:6

"Pray at all times in the Spirit, with all prayer and supplication. To that end keep alert with all perseverance."
—Ephesians 6:18

"We pray best when we are no longer aware of praying."
—Cassian

"The main purpose of prayer is not to make life easier, nor to gain magical powers, but to know God."

—Philip Yancey, *Prayer: Does It Make Any Difference?*

Writing a chapter on prayer reminds me of something that R. C. Sproul said when writing a book on the holiness of God. He said, "It's dangerous to assume that because a person is drawn to holiness in his study that he is thereby a holy man. There is irony here. I am sure the reason I have a deep hunger to learn of the holiness of God is precisely because I am not holy" (*The Holiness of God*, R. C. Sproul, pg. 33). I understand the sentiment. I feel much the same way when it comes to writing on prayer.

Prayer is one of those practices that we know we should engage in more often but find that we do not make time nor discipline ourselves to do so. We make time to watch three to four hours (or more) of football, three to four hours to watch a World Series game, or hours upon hours to watch mindless TV shows, and then complain that we just can't find the time to pray because we are "so busy." And understand, I am not pointing fingers. I wish I could tell you just how many worthless hours I have spent watching golf, Cowboy, or Texas Aggie football games. Or other mindless hours of TV viewing.

One of the concepts I have come across over the years has been the concept of "practical atheism." What this actually means is that those of us who call ourselves Christians live as if God does not exist, even though our lips say that He does. One of the ways this finds expression is in the ways we do not pray.

If we were to be real with one another, I think we would agree that there are several reasons or justifications we give for not praying as we should. One, we say that life has just become so harried and complicated that we have a hard time finding time to pray. Another is that we are not really sure that God answers prayer, or at least in the ways we think that He should, so we just don't bother Him. Third, I find that we all ask the question, at least from time to time, what difference does prayer make? A fourth reason is that we think we must "assume the position" (knees bent, head bowed) in order for prayer to be "real" prayer. All prayer that doesn't meet these posture positions is not really prayer at all, or so we think.

I have found that, as my bones and muscles have aged along with the rest of me, were I to be on bended knee every time I pray, I would probably need help getting up because either (a) circulation to my lower extremities has been cut off, or (b) my knee caps have cracked, and surgery is needed immediately!

The questions that remain when we are talking about prayer are questions that we often ask. What is prayer? What good is prayer? Why should we pray if God is sovereign? Does prayer really change anything? Are there certain positions we should take when praying? How often should we pray? How long should we pray? Who and what is prayer for? What types of prayers are we to pray? Is it okay to ask for "stuff"? When we pray for healings, why is everyone not healed? Why do we not pray more? The list of questions we could ask is endless, but I will end with this final one: Why do we seem to pray only when we need something or are in trouble?

It was never my plan to approach this chapter on prayer from the customary approaches I have read or heard taken. Prayer is very serious business, yet so many of the treatments of prayer leave me feeling defeated already or they leave me with a very dry sense of what prayer actually should be. Every single Christian I have ever known struggles with prayer, and most feel guilty that we don't seem to pray enough. I would love to say that this chapter will alleviate that guilt, but the truth is that we probably don't pray enough. I know that I do not, and only because of talking with others do I have any sense of confidence that we live in a mutual-lack-of-praying society within our hallowed walls.

PRAYER AND PRAYING

Watching as much sports as I have watched over the years, I have seen athletes "thank God" or "thank Jesus" when they have just won a really close or hard fought contest, and while I appreciate the sentiment, I have often wondered what the Christians on the other team might be thinking. Does the God who answers prayer only answer the prayers of the winners? I have yet to see the athlete who says, "I just want to thank God for letting us lose," as if God were picking sides in these contests, and "let" anyone win or lose.

I pondered this one day when I was thinking about first and second century Rome, and the gladiator contests and the games in which Christians were fed to the lions for sport. As Christians who were about to become dinner, they prayed, "Father, forgive them," I wondered how our modern athletic competitors would react to such heartfelt and final prayer? The truth is, I wondered how I would react in the same situation. I realized that the early Christians could pray that way because prayer was the warp and woof of their lives. It was a common, everyday occurrence.

So what is prayer actually? How does one define prayer in such a way that it is both meaningful and biblical (not that these two are mutually exclusive)? How do we pray in such a way that honors God and is more than just bringing Him a laundry list of requests we want fulfilled? These and other such questions are the questions I ponder when considering prayer and how we define prayer and how we pray.

Prayer tends to be a monologue, meaning that we usually talk and expect God to be the benevolent counselor who listens while we talk. But somehow, this falls short of what prayer is and should be.

The term "prayer" can also be used as a convenient way of saying something without saying anything. How many times have we read or heard someone say or said ourselves, "You are in my thoughts and prayers." This is almost like politicians saying, after a political speech, "God bless you and God bless America!" It sounds good. It feels good. It resonates with many. But I am reminded of the college newspaper editorial from many years ago that was shared with us at a conference in Colorado. The writer wrote about how he and others liked G.O.D., except that he meant it for an acronym "Get Off Daily," referring to their current consumption of weed. Not that people are always insincere when saying what they do. But I can say with some amount of authority that I am not sure I have always then prayed when I told someone that "you are in my thoughts and prayers." As Lemuel Tucker, a young speaker at the Urbana Missions Conference in 1976, so aptly said, "And don't get caught up in half-truths by telling everyone you are praying for them. Learn to be obedient within the daily routine of prayer" (Lemuel Tucker, "Declare His Glory On The Campus"; Urbana Missions Conference, Urbana, Il. December 1976).

This point was driven home to me one Sunday when my oldest daughter, Jennifer, and I were driving to my hometown that morning, and I decided to turn on the radio to hear my former college roommate preach. The church where he was pastor had their morning services broadcast over the local radio station, so I decided we would listen in. As we listened, he began to tell the story of how, during the first six weeks of college, he and his roommate (that would be me) just could not get along and seemed to bicker often to the point of constant irritation. I turned to my daughter and said, "That's true. We really had a rough first six weeks." He continued. "Well, I will tell you what we did. We got down on our knees and prayed! And things got better." At this point, I turned to my daughter again and said, "He's lying." She just broke out laughing (even at her young age, she had a great sense of humor!). I explained that neither he nor I hardly touched the doors of a church that first year and certainly had very little idea of prayer other than "Help!" when taking our first exams! I have jokingly said for years that I attended the "Church of the Hidden Springs" that first year; I slept in most Sunday mornings.

I saw him later that afternoon and told him I had heard his sermon that morning. "You did, eh?" he said. "Yeah, I did," I replied. I asked him what exactly did he mean by saying "we prayed," when what we really did was to sit down and talk through some things to clear the air about the things bothering us. "Well, let's say 'pastoral license' to make a point. The sermon was on prayer." I laughed and said, "Yeah, I got that part, but your pastoral license stretched it there a bit!"

I don't tell the story to put him in a bad light but to point out how we sometimes say things about prayer and praying that just are not true! He is not the only person to ever take "pastoral license" about prayer; we have all done it in some form or fashion.

So what then is prayer? How are we to "not talk" but listen to the voice of the Master?

Prayer: More Than a Monologue

Praying should involve for us at least four elements that Scripture mentions. These four are confession, thankfulness, petitioning, and praise.

I will make this very simple. Confession is simply confessing or admitting to sin or sins and asking for God's forgiveness. Thankfulness is simply being thankful for whatever God lays on your heart and especially for His grace and mercy. Petitioning is simply speaking with God about those things that you are needing (daily bread, etc.) and that are on your mind. This is also where interceding prayer for others would be found. Finally, praise is simply that: praise for who God is, what He has done, and what He will continue to do.

Rather than go into some long explanation and a theological treatise on what each of these are, simplicity rules the day. Books have been written about each of these "elements," but they are not actually that complicated. John Ortberg writes, "In simple prayer, I pray about what is really on my heart, not what I wish was on my heart… nothing kills prayer faster than when I pretend in prayer to be more noble than I really am" (*The Life You've Always Wanted*, pg. 100). He goes on to quote Dallas Willard, who says, "Prayer simply *dies* from efforts to pray about 'good things' that honestly do not matter to us. The way to get to meaningful prayer for those good things is to start by praying for what we are truly interested in" (pg. 100).

The most difficult part of prayer is praying. As Bloesch reminds us, "We often fail to realize that the hardest work of all is prayer" (Bloesch, *Crumbling Foundations*, pg.136). This sounds almost contradictory, but let me ask you: does your mind ever wander in prayer? Mine certainly does. While I am trying to pray for world peace and all missionaries, I find myself thinking about that dropped pass or that missed putt or images that I would like to shake from my conscious mind that shouldn't be there but seem to rise to prominence just at the time I should be praising. Prayer is simple but oh so difficult.

If our minds aren't wandering, we can get distracted by the least of noises or the least of other distractions. We develop "dog ears" while we pray, hearing sounds that we normally would not hear in our normal routine and that are usually inaudible to the human ear. So when we pray, we need to find and develop a place where we will have the least amount of distractions.

This, of course, brings us to the next obstacle we face in prayer, and that is simply staying awake! At my age, I have found that I have a tendency to get up more during the night than I did when I was younger. Bladders don't wait, and they call more often, so the result is sleep deprivation. Even without this challenge, our culture tends to be sleep deprived and this raises its ugly head when we slow down long enough to pray. So make it a point to get enough sleep, whatever that may be for you.

Prayer is more than simply a monologue, however. It is more than confessing, thanking, petitioning, and praising. Sometimes (and perhaps more than we allow), it is simply listening and meditating, both to God's Word and the Holy Spirit as He speaks to us in His own way. I am not speaking of an audible voice, for few have actually ever heard His voice, but He does speak to us both within and outside of ourselves, if we are quiet enough to listen. I formerly believed and have read that prayer was a "dialogue," and sometimes that is the case. Certainly, Abraham, Moses, and Gideon had dialogues in their prayers with God. But it is more than just dialogue with the Heavenly Father. If I am wise, I will spend more time just listening than any other prayer activity that I do.

TWO SIMPLE GUIDES TO PRAYING

There have been legions of books written on prayer that are excellent. *Prayer* by O. Hallesby is one of the classics. Others have been written with instructions on how to pray if you are a woman, if you are a businessman, if you are busy, and the last one I have read, *Prayer: Does It Make Any Difference?* by Philip Yancey. All have different things to say about prayer and are written by those who have studied and practiced prayer and had many of the same struggles and questions we all have had.

In meditating on this topic, it occurred to me that we have been given several examples of prayer in Scripture, but two serve as prime examples of the beauty of the simplicity of prayer or how prayer can and should be simple.

Jesus gave us an example of how to pray and had a very pointed reason when He gave it to us in Matthew 6:5–13. The first point He is making is to not pray as the hypocrites do, who did it to be seen by men. Second, He says not to pray as the Gentiles do, who pray a long time, thinking that their many words will count for something (perhaps wearing down the Lord with their length!) We have all heard someone pray for a long time (perhaps we have even done it ourselves!), thinking that by doing so, he or she may at least sound more spiritual because of the length of the prayer. I have been reminded on occasion to "please not catch up on my prayer life when praying over the meal."

The prayer that Jesus gives us is simple and is as follows:

> Our Father who are in heaven, Hallowed be Thy name. Thy kingdom come, Thy will be done, on earth as it is in heaven. Give us this day our daily bread. And forgive us our trespasses, as we forgive those who trespass against us. And do not lead us into temptation, but deliver us from evil. For Thine is the kingdom, and thepower, and the glory, forever. Amen. (Matthew 6:9–13)

It doesn't get much simpler than this. We are to acknowledge our God who is holy and to pray for His will, both on earth as in heaven. We are to ask for daily sustenance, and we are to practice forgiveness. We are to ask not to be tempted or led to do evil and to acknowledge His kingdom, His power, and His glory eternally. This prayer that Jesus gives us is both simple and short and yet powerful in its simplicity. If you and I acknowledged all we are told we should, had daily "bread," lived in total forgiveness, and did not commit any evil, that would just about cover it, don't you think? In the grand scheme of life, in the broader view of life, don't these basic themes cover all that is really important in life?

Philip Yancey writes in his book *Prayer: Does It Make Any Difference?*: "I have a friend in Japan who provides resources to the underground church in China and often worships among them. One day I asked her, 'How do Chinese Christians pray? Do their prayers differ from what you hear in the U.S. or Japan?' She replied that the prayers closely follow the pattern of the Lord's Prayer. The church has spread most widely among the lower classes, and when they ask for daily bread and deliverance from evil, they mean it literally" (Yancey, *Prayer*, pg. 238).

The second guide to prayer comes from *Psalm 51* in the Old Testament. It is the heartfelt prayer of David after he has been caught committing adultery with Bathsheba and sending her husband off to the frontlines to, in essence, be killed so that David would have some justification in his own mind over what he had done. All of the Psalm would be an excellent guide for prayer, but I would like to focus on verses 10–13. It reads as follows:

> Create in me a clean heart, O God. And, renew a stead-fast spirit within me. Do not cast me away from Thy presence, And do not take Thy Holy Spirit from me. Restore to me the joy of Thy salvation, And sustain me with a willing spirit. Then I will teach transgressors Thy ways, And sinners will be converted to Thee.

While the prayer that Jesus teaches us focuses on God and in having Him acknowledged and meeting immediate personal needs, David's prayer of repentance focuses on deep, personal sin and the longing to have that sin forgiven and to "create" a clean heart.

I cannot speak for everyone reading this, but it is probably a fairly safe assumption that most have not murdered or sinned in the ways that David sinned. It is also a safe assumption that all of us have sinned in ways that have been hurtful to others and hurtful toward God, and in some cases, a very deep type of hurtful sin was committed. There are personal sins I have committed that will stay between me and God, but I can say without a doubt that these sins have hurt others and have hurt God. I have, through tears, prayed this very prayer on more than one occasion and asked for the same cleansing that David is asking for. Because of the basic nature of human beings, it is why this prayer is so very important for us to have this as a guide.

Now this is not a prayer we pray every day (or at least, I would hope not!). But confessing sin in such a deep, personal way is something we should always be aware of, for those of us who struggle with what and how to pray, it serves as another very simple but profound guide in praying.

The words from the title of the song for this chapter say the following:

> Don't talk, put your head on my shoulder. Don't talk, close your eyes and be still. Don't talk, put your head on my shoulder. And listen to my heartbeat. Listen, listen, listen.

While prayer involves all I have written about in this chapter, perhaps nothing could be more profound than to just pray so as to *listen* to God's heartbeat and get in step with just what that is. *"Listen, listen, listen."*

CHAPTER 5

I'm Waiting for the Day

"There is no pre-hell, post-hell, or a-hell."
—Dr. Earl Radmacher
(chapel service, Western Seminary, 1979)

"Heaven and earth will pass away, but My words shall not pass away. But of that day and hour no one knows, not even the angels of heaven, nor the Son, but the Father alone."
—Matthew 24:35–36

"Pre-, post-, and amillennialism are relatively modern terms. Thus one must be careful not to impose them on earlier ages."
—Richard Kyle, *The Last Days Are Here Again*

"Warning: In case of rapture, this car will be left unmanned."
—Bumper sticker on cars in 1970s

"In my years of study and ministry I have yet
to discover a single text of sacred Scripture that
teaches a pretribulation Rapture. In my opinion
the notion, which is quite recent in church history, is pure fiction."

—R. C. Sproul, Foreword to:
End Times Fiction, Gary DeMar

"And because lawlessness is increased, most people's love will grow cold."

—Jesus Christ, Matthew 24: 12

"I'm waiting for the day when you can love again."

—Brian Wilson/Tony Asher

One of the great interests of our time is an interest with the future.
The popularity of such interest wanes at times, like the ebb and flow
of the ocean currents, but people, generally, have seemed to have
always held a fascination with what the future holds and, particularly,
their futures!

Turn on your television sets and on any given station (and there
are now hundreds of them), someone is alluring you to call this 800
number and speak with a real, live psychic. Of course, it is couched
in terms of money and romance primarily so as to appeal to our base
instincts. The implication is who wouldn't like to know about their
future financial situations or their future romantic connections? So
the appeal to know one's future becomes an alluring web.

In biblical terms and in the world of theology, the study of future
things or prophecy is termed *eschatology*. The Bible is full of passages
alluding to or predicting future events. Primary among those teachings is the teaching on the Second Coming of Jesus Christ. Much of

the focus of prophetic study is given to those things Jesus said would be "signs" of His coming again.

I am not a prophetic scholar. Literally, volumes have been written that are of a scholarly nature in the field of eschatology. However, what I hope to do with this chapter is shed some light on the differing ways that the study of future things, eschatology, is taught. And the focus will be on the differing views of the millennium since this is where most eschatological studies take us anyway. This is a primer, after all, and an introduction to those things in Christian thought, which have often been taught in such a way that we come out the other side in a fog. My goal is to clear up *some* of the fog.

LATE GREAT AND LEFT BEHIND

My initial introduction to prophecy came in the form of Hal Lindsey's best-selling book of the 1970s, *The Late Great Planet Earth*. This book has sold over thirty million copies and was the New York Times best-selling book of the decade of the 1970s. Like many others at the time, I had no idea what the book was about, but the title was intriguing. So I bought a copy in 1970 and began reading.

This book and its sequel, *There's A New World Coming*, were attempts to put prophetic teachings found primarily in the books of Daniel, Ezekiel, Matthew, and Revelation in modern contexts and with modern interpretations. In other words, they described allegorical and symbolic images in terms of current politics and current military weaponry. Armageddon at your doorstep! I had no idea of the particular theological grid through which these interpretations were being made; it just made for interesting reading for me at the time.

These books introduced me to the study of prophecy and to the world of what I later came to know as "Eschatology." In the world of seminarians and the world of theological studies, sooner or later, one is introduced to what is called Systematic Theology. Within this world, theology is "systematized" into different areas of study. Rather than giving you a rundown at this point, I would refer you to the appendix at the back of the book where I have listed what are these actual areas of study.[1] But one of those areas of study is Eschatology.

In reading and studying prophecy, I began to realize that not everyone agreed and some even went so far as to get really specific about either the date or the general time frame in which Christ was to return. For example, Lindsey initially worked his timeframe within about a forty-year stretch, beginning with the creation of the nation of Israel as a state in 1948. Others such as Edgar Whisenhunt had somehow mathematically "figured out the formula" as to when Christ would return, and in his booklet *88 Reasons Why the Rapture Will Be in 1988* set the specific dates of between September 11 and 13, 1988 as to when the rapture would take place. Of course, we are still here, so he shockingly missed it by, oh, at least twenty-five years (if, indeed, such a thing as the rapture is actually biblically true). I bought his booklet and read it back at the time and must admit, it sounded very convincing except for one rather major flaw. Jesus, Himself, had said that *no one* would know the day or hour, and it can be safely assumed that the "no one" included Mr. Whisenhunt. And anyone else who has attempted to put a date or timeframe on His return. But we can rest assure that others will come along and try to pinpoint a date. Such is our curiosity and folly of wanting to name a date and know the future. And as comedian Ron White might say, "You can't fix stupid!"

In rolling the calendar forward a few decades, the blockbuster series of books by Tim LaHaye and Jerry Jenkins hit the bookstands and have sold millions. The initial book in the series we know as *Left Behind*. A movie starring Kirk Cameron was made called *Left Behind* (imagine that) and was mass-produced to sell to the public. This book and the ones in this series, which followed, were all works of fiction and were one man's fictionalized stories of what he imagined would happen in the aftermath of the rapture.

While publicized as a work of fiction, it sold in the millions and became the next generation's *Late Great Planet Earth*, except that Lindsey's book *read* like fiction but is not, while LaHaye's book actually is fiction. R. C. Sproul had this to say in this regard: "The *Left Behind* series is clearly fiction. But it involves the literary genre of fiction to teach a theological viewpoint that the authors do not believe is fiction" (DeMar, Foreword, pg. viii, *End Times Fiction*). Crucial to understanding the impact of these books, their purposes were evangelistic and have been used to bring people to Christ. That is the good news.

What needs to be understood about these books, however, is that they are written with a particular theological interpretation of Scripture, one based on a premillennial dispensational interpretation of Scripture. This is important to know because not all would agree that this particular interpretation is actually correct, and that some who oppose this view believe that thousands are being led astray.

HERMENEUTICS: THE ART AND SCIENCE OF BIBLICAL INTERPRETATION

I had the distinct pleasure of teaching an adult Sunday morning Bible study at my church for almost eight years. On occasion, I threw out words such as *hermeneutics* just so I could remind them that I did know a few words that are multisyllabic! I will define it for our purposes here shortly.

One of the things that I constantly stressed in this class was to understand that all of us read Scripture through our own grids. Our pasts, our backgrounds, our experiences tend to be the grids through which we "see" Scripture, and it is important that we keep that ever so clearly in mind. As much as we would like to think that we read and study Scripture objectively, the truth is that much subjectivity goes into reading and studying the Bible.

Hermeneutics is one of those terms that sounds doctoral in the manner in which it is spoken and used. My class saw it enough that they indulged me when I wrote it on the board. It means, in the strictest sense of the word, the "science of biblical interpretation." It is how we are to study and understand what the biblical writers meant. It is how we get to as much objectivity as is humanly possible.

Why this section on hermeneutics? First of all, because it is my book and I chose to put it in here! Seriously, however, understanding that hermeneutics goes into what serious theologians and scholars try to do when interpreting Scripture will help us to understand something about how systems of interpreting come into play when studying prophecy. There are a wealth of books that have been written going into great detail to explain and teach hermeneutics, so that is not my purpose here. I simply want to introduce hermeneutics to you so that you can at least be familiar with the term and to get a thumbnail sketch of how hermeneutics is used in addressing the differing theological systems that produce the four differing views of the millennium.

T. Norton Sterrett has written a great book entitled *How to Understand Your Bible,* published by Inter-Varsity Press. I would encourage those of you reading this to purchase this book if you are interested in having a good volume that explains hermeneutics in very readable terms. He goes into much greater detail than I will here.

When reading the Bible and trying to interpret and understand what is being said, I always remember something one of my seminary professors said to our class. His exact comment was, "The Bible doesn't mean what it says. The Bible means what it means." That is hermeneutics in a very precise nutshell.

Several concepts have to be kept in mind when reading and understanding the Bible. First of all, *context* is important. The context of the passage being read within the immediate chapter, within the book in which it was written, and within the testament in which it was written. Historical and cultural context are important as is the context within the whole of both New and Old Testaments. Second, the history of the significant words being used in the passage is important. This is known as *etymology*. Third, *who is the writer or speaker* and what is his current situation? (In Paul's case, several of his letters were written from prison, so this helps to understand some of the terminology he uses.) Fourth, *the Bible is its own interpreter*. One passage will throw light on another. This is quite important in light of the fact that some passages seem to contradict other ones when they are taken completely out of context. James Sire deals with this in detail in his book, *Scripture Twisting*. It is how we end up with the Jim Jones of this world, who take great liberties with Scripture and use them for their own ends. We have all known of those who try to prove anything by using Scripture to prove their points. I have even read books written by atheists who use Scripture to prove their points, and they isolate passages *way* out of context to make their points.

There are other important factors involved in interpreting Scripture such as symbols, types, parables, allegorical language, poetic language, and idioms, and volumes have been written about these as well. Not to be forgotten in all of this is a dependence upon the Holy Spirit to guide us into all truth. This doesn't mean study and the concepts mentioned are not important. The Holy Spirit cannot guide a docked ship, no matter how often the rudder is turned!

What hermeneutics comes down to is interpreting Scripture as best as we can, using the tools that are available to do so. But we have to use the tools! Another of those big theological terms we have either seen in print or have heard is *exegesis*. To *exegete* a passage is to interpret that passage in light of all the aforementioned tools available. Where people like Jim Jones get in trouble is when they do what is termed *eisegesis*.

That is, they *isolate* passages way out of context to either support or "prove" the point they are trying to make.

What, you may be asking, has any of this to do with prophecy and the Second Coming of Christ? Sterrett says, "One writer has said that in the study of prophecy the Bible student finds some of the greatest problems of interpretation." He goes on to say that, "We recognize that there is a great difference of conviction about Bible prophecy, yet prophecy, especially the predictions about Christ's first and second coming, is one of the most important parts of the Bible" (Sterrett, *How to Understand Your Bible*, pg. 140).

It is these differences to which we turn and which are important to know so that when a speaker, pastor, or teacher is heard speaking on this subject, you may have some idea of the manner in which he or she has gone about looking at Scripture. In other words, what theological grid is being used to interpret one's view of eschatology?

THE FOUR VIEWS OF THE MILLENNIUM

Before I begin this section, I must say that I began this chapter with one of my favorite quotes I have ever heard spoken on this subject. Dr. Earl Radmacher, who was president of Western Seminary in Portland, Oregon, when I attended there, was speaking to the student body one day in chapel. Dr. Radmacher had written on behalf of and was a proponent of the view that has become dominant in our churches over the last one hundred years, pre-millennial dispensationalist. Many a Christian has gotten so wrapped up in arguing for his or her theological system that Dr. Radmacher wanted to drive home his point in a clear, concise, and effective way. He was making it clear that evangelism and taking the gospel to all nations was the point, and to emphasize that point, with all of us clearly knowing what his particular view was, he said, "Let me be clear. There is no pre-hell, post-hell, or a-hell." In other words, don't get so wrapped up in the differing views that you miss the point!

I would say the same thing here. While it is important to know what these views are, they are not the main point. Knowing them will help to discern what is behind what someone is teaching or preaching, and that is always helpful.

I am not listing these in any particular order of importance or significance. In other words, though I have my own particular bias, my purpose here is to simply state what the differing views are, without any order of preference or importance.

Also, one of the key points for understanding eschatology and millennial views is how Israel and the Church are viewed. This is not only key, it is actually crucial to how one then understands the conclusions one comes to in determining how one understands what the Bible teaches about the end times, and such things as the teachings on a Tribulation, a rapture, a thousand-year reign, and the distinction between the views taken of Israel (national? Spiritual? What?) and the Church (distinct from Israel? Continuation of the covenant with Israel? Fulfillment of the covenant with Israel? What?). To quote Abraham Lincoln, "Good men disagree."

View Number One: Amillennialism. Amillennialism, according to many who have studied the history of eschatological views, has been the predominate view for much of Christian history. In simplest terms, amillennialists "do not believe that Christ will establish a literal earthly rule before the judgment. Rather, the glorious new heaven and earth will immediately follow the present dispensation of the kingdom of God" (Richard Kyle, *The Last Days Are Here Again*, pg. 21). In other words, they hold to the "belief that there will not be a literal 1000 year reign of Christ." "The amillennialist assumes that most, or all, unfulfilled prophecy is written in symbolic, figurative, spiritual language." According to some, they use what is termed a "dual hermeneutic" (see, I told you that hermeneutics was important!) whereby "non-prophetic Scripture and fulfilled prophecy are interpreted literally or normally, and unfulfilled prophecy is to be interpreted spiritually, or non-literally" (What Is Amillennialism?, www.gotquestions.org).

Generally, the amillennial view holds that most of prophecy has already been fulfilled, and most of that fulfillment occurred before AD 70. A view taken by R. C. Sproul and others is called "preterist," which I believe would fall under the amillennial view and has most of prophecy fulfilled by this date, including the Second Coming of Christ. This view holds that Christ is already ruling (the thousand-year symbolic reign) on His throne and came again around the time of the destruction of the temple in Jerusalem near AD 70. While this view may have been held for most of Christian history, it is certainly not the dominant view that is held most widely today. That doesn't prove it or other views right or wrong, just that this is not what most in the church are taught or believe today.

It is also important to note that one the of main distinctions, and at the same time, one of the main points of difference that this view holds as opposed to other millennial views is the amillennialist's view of Israel and the church. This interpretation is predominantly a "Covenant Theology" view, in which the Church of the New Testament is seen as a continuation of Israel of the Old Testament. This is based on a view that sees the "Covenants" of the Old Testament as being fulfilled by the covenant of the New Testament, which is fulfilled in Jesus Christ and His death and resurrection. There are entire books written about this view, so what you are getting here is a really brief summary. I would encourage additional reading on this, in particular, *A Case for Amillennialism*, written by Kim Riddlebarger.

View Number Two: Historic Premillennialsim. Before defining this view as clearly as is possible, it is significant to note that all who hold to some sort of premillennial view believe that the tribulation period is followed by one thousand years of peace when all live under the authority of Christ. Afterward, Satan is permanently defeated in a final battle, and a new heaven and a new earth are established. Whether one believes in historic or dispensational or any other premillennial view that exists, the thousand-year reign is common to all views.

Having said that, the best way it seems to define historic premillennialism is by comparing it to its premillenial counterpoint, dispensationalist (which I will deal with later in this chapter).

According to website www.gotquestions.org, "Historic premillennialism was held by a large majority of Christians during the first three centuries of the Christian era." It was "declared a heresy at the Council of Ephesus in 431 A.D." and was "suppressed." While this is true, it also appears that those who espouse the view that it was suppressed are doing so to push forth their own agendas. Nonetheless and in spite of this, several noted scholars of the twentieth century have adopted the historic premillennial view, such as George Eldon Ladd, John Warwick Montgomery, J. Barton Payne, and Walter Martin.

The historic view teaches that "the church was in the fore-vision of the Old Testament prophecy, while dispensationalist teaches that the church is hardly, if at all, mentioned by the Old Testament prophets." It also teaches that the "present age of grace was designed by God and predicted in the Old Testament," whereas dispensationalist's views hold that "the present age was unforeseen in the Old Testament and thus is a 'great parenthesis' introduced because the Jews rejected the kingdom." Finally (and this is key), the historic view teaches that "one may divide time in any way desirable so long as one allows for a millennium after the second coming. Dispensationalism maintains that the only allowable way to divide time is into seven dispensations."

As do most who hold to a premillenial view, a "rapture" of the church is taught with this view, which says that Jesus and His Church will return to earth to rule for a millennium. Proponents of the rapture have broken into several camps, including pretribulation rapture, post-tribulation rapture, mid-tribulation rapture, pre-wrath rapture, and a partial rapture! A virtual smorgasbord of rapture views, all backed up with Scriptural references. This is why the study of hermeneutics is so important.

How, one may ask, can there be so many divergent views of an event that even educated theologians cannot agree on, and that some would hold is not an event at all! It is all about hermeneutics and the assumptions with which one begins as to where one will end. Even good people do not agree, but that is okay.

View Number Three: Dispensational Premillenialism. The dispensational view is the "new kid on the block" in strictly historic terms. This view was first taught by J. N. B. Darby in the nineteenth century and was later popularized through the influential teachings of C. I. Scofield. One of the first Bibles I received was from a former fifth grade school teacher, and it was a Scofield reference Bible, complete with dispensational interpretative footnotes. Richard Kyle writes, "While the historicist premillennialists were wedded to an exact millennial arithmetic, the dispensationalists lived with 'maybes'" (Kyle, *The Last Days Are Here Again*, pg.103).

This view was further popularized through the influences of Lewis Sperry Chafer and his seminary, Dallas Theological Seminary or DTS. Many of the theological works heavily influencing this teaching came from the minds and the pens of professors at this seminary, including John Walvoord, J. Dwight Pentecost, and Charles Ryrie. The largest influence by far came, however, from Hal Lindsey and his book *The Late Great Planet Earth*. Lindsey was a graduate of DTS and took the views he was taught and popularized them. It is also this view that is behind the series *Left Behind.*

It is the dominant view in our churches today, by a wide margin. This is especially so in Bible churches, nondenominational churches, and conservative Baptist and evangelical churches. Anyone teaching differently from this view is thought to be teaching heresy, or so it seems. Considering that this view is relatively young in the history of the church, the speed with which this view has taken hold in our churches is an interesting phenomenon in itself.

So what is this view, and what does it teach?

First of all, Dispensationalism teaches a clear distinction between Israel and the church in God's program. This view holds that God's promises to Israel in the Old Testament have not been transferred to the church of the New Testament, and that He will fulfill His promises to Israel in the thousand-year reign of Christ on the earth.

Second, it teaches a distinct and clear breaking down of history into seven "dispensations," thus "Dispensationalism." The church age becomes a "parentheses" or "parenthetical" in this distinctive teaching. This is very important in understanding how dispensationalists explain the existence of the church and the parenthetical place it holds in history, according to their views.

It is important to note that those who adhere to dispensational teaching also believe that they have the distinctive of holding a consistently literal interpretation of Scripture, especially Bible prophecy. "Dispensationalists claim that their principle of hermeneutics [there is that word again!] is that of literal interpretation" and that "if literal interpretation is not used in studying the Scriptures, there is no objective standard by which to understand the Bible" (www.gotquestions.org).

There is obviously much more to the teachings of dispensational thought as well as millennialism and historic premillennism than I will be able to show here. It is important to know the distinctions of all of the views so that you may decide for yourself, which system seems to be truest to the biblical text. With that in mind, we will proceed to the fourth millennial view, post-millennialism.

View Number Four: Post-Millennialism. The fourth and final view we will consider has as its cornerstone belief that Christ's Second Coming occurs *after* the millennium, which will be a golden age of Christian prosperity and dominance. Though not totally aligned with this view, religious writers such as R. J. Rushdoony, Gary North, and Greg Bahnsen, and their Reconstructionist view of history would have agreed with a golden age of Christian dominance, advocating a theocratic government based on Old Testament law.

Richard Kyle writes that, "In 1860 the majority of American Protestants embraced postmillennialiam, but by the early twentieth century it had largely disappeared" (Richard Kyle, *The Last Days Are Here Again*, pg. 102). Post-Millennialism "is the belief that Christ returns after a period of time, but not necessarily a literal 1000 years." Those holding this view believe that Revelation 20:4–6 should not be taken literally, but that one thousand years simply means a "long period of time." Also, germane to this view is that Christians themselves will have established the kingdom of God on this earth before the return of Christ. The bottom line for this view is that those who adopt this view believe that the world will just keep getting better and better, that the world will become Christianized, and that the utopia we would all love to experience will actually come to be before the return of Christ.

In other words, the millennial kingdom will be established by the church and not by Christ Himself.

It needs to be understood that I am giving a sweeping overview of all of these views of the millennium. There are other branches on this tree of millennial teaching that I have neither the expertise nor the inclination to get into for our purposes here. Each one has advocates that fully believe that their particular hermeneutical approach and conclusions are biblically correct. While the study of and knowledge of these views is helpful, we should not get bogged down and be at odds with one another when we disagree on millennial views. There is even one view which is referred to as "pan-millennialism," meaning everything will "pan out" in the long run. For obvious reasons, that one is self explanatory.

Kyle says in his well-written book *The Last Days Are Here Again*, "In respect to end-time thinking, two common mistakes are made. On the one hand, some Christians have become obsessed with it, especially the chronology of Christ's return. On the other hand, Christians pay scant attention to Bible prophecy" (Kyle, pg. 198). He further communicates an important insight into some of the problems we encounter with the end-times speculations. He writes:

> Eschatology is a broad subject. Unfortunately, end-time thinking focuses primarily on only one aspect of it – the chronology of the end. The order of events surrounding Christ's return is not the most important dimension in the Christian teaching regarding the end of the world. Yet, it has taken center stage. Why? Humans crave to know the future, and in particular when the end will come. (Kyle, pg. 198)

As I have often said (and my wife can attest to this, as could have my Sunday School class, who both heard me say this so many times that I could see eyes roll when I started), there are three things we know for certain about the second coming of Christ (and thus, the millennium). First, we know He is coming back. Second, we know we don't know when He is coming back. Third, we know we are to be as ready as possible.

Those three things we know for sure. And rather than get into a tizzy about wondering and worrying about when all of this is to take place, it would be helpful to remember the response of D. L. Moody, nineteenth century evangelist and preacher, to a question in this regard. Legend has it that he was asked, "Mr. Moody, if you knew Christ were returning tomorrow, what would you do?" His response was both refreshing and unexpected. "I would plant a tree," he said. Something of this nature of response is also attributed to St. Francis of Asissi. In other words, I would keep on doing what I am doing! *That* is how to be ready! That is how to be "waiting for the day."

Now for those who would like to pursue further study on this particular area of interest, I would recommend two books, which go into greater detail of the views of the millennium. These books are *The Meaning of the Millennium: Four Views* (edited by Robert Clouse and published by Inter-Varsity Press), *Three Views on the Millennium and Beyond* (edited by Darrel Bock, published by Zondervan). Richard Kyle's book *The Last Days are Here Again* (Baker House Books) is also an excellent overview of the "history of the end times."

I cannot end this chapter without saying that the study of prophecy is one in which we should be careful as to how we hold the views we hold. More dissension seems to arise from opposing views in this area of belief than just about any other area within the church. Each view has its proponents, and each view has its merits. We need to live with each other and with those who do not hold to our views without crucifying them or getting nasty when we don't agree. Mention that you believe the teaching of the rapture and watch those who don't agree attack! Mention that you don't believe that the rapture is a biblical teaching and watch those who do believe this attack! We must hold to what we believe with love and without attacking those who do not hold to that same belief. And remember, "There is no pre-hell, post-hell or a-hell!"

CHAPTER 6

Let's Go Away For a While

"The trouble with being in the rat race is that even if you win, you're still a rat."
—Lily Tomlin

"We're stampeding toward the cliff. Exhausted and breathless, we Sprint, Quicken, FedEx, Twitter, and text. And the things that make our lives rich are lost in the blur.
—Phil Callaway,
Making Your Life Rich without Any Money

"To do anything well, you must have time off from it. Time away from constantly doing it. Time to recover and relax. Time to do something else. Time to just forget about it."
—Al Gini, *The Importance of Being Lazy*

"It's a five o'clock world and the whistle blows. No one owns a piece of my time."
—The Vogues, *Five O'clock World*

"I do not like work, even when someone else
does it."

—Mark Twain

Flying is probably not at the top of the list of favorite things I like
to do. Fact is, it doesn't really make the list. Nonetheless, through
the years of working for different companies, I have had meetings
planned that required flying to those meetings. One such meeting
took place in Orlando, Florida, home of Disney World, the Orlando
Magic, and the Epcot Center. None of those things, however, made
it on our agenda. Mostly, I saw the inside of the hotel, the meeting rooms, and the scenery from and back to the airport. I am sure
Orlando is the magical place that Disney advertises; it is just that I
never saw that part of Orlando. The most magical thing I saw were
the glass elevators which, if you have a fear of heights, allowed you to
experience that fear while speeding to the top of the hotel!

The flight back from Orlando, however, allowed me the privilege of sitting next to a person who turned out to be a professor at
the University of Florida. Her subject? Leisure. I am not making this
up. She was on her way to a resort in Colorado to do, as she put it,
"research." Now I don't know about you, but that sounded really
close to being like, oh I don't know, a dream job! "Research" involved
spending time at various vacation and resort locations around the
globe and was paid for by the university or the resort requesting that
such research be done at their location. Wow… what a deal!

A major in *leisure* was not on any curriculum guide that I saw
when I attended college. In fact, no such major existed on most college courses of study until the last few years. So being the curious
and envious type that I am, I was full of questions for the professor.
"How," I asked, "did you come about finding a place that had such a
course of study?" Her undergraduate major, if I remember correctly,
was in recreation, but as she proceeded forward with her post-gradu-

ate degrees, she was able to pursue this course of study. It seems that Florida is the ideal place to pursue such a course, as retirees flock there for leisure, and studies were needed to determine what people did for leisure, why they did it, where they went and why, who they went with, what appealed to them and what did not, and on and on with such statistical studies. *Where*, I thought, *was this when I was attending college?*

VACATIONS AND LEISURE IN CHILDHOOD

Part of my fascination with leisure and vacations and why the conversation was so interesting to me was the fact that I did not take vacations as a child and have not taken that many as an adult.

My dad worked as a postal employee, and my mom worked in retail shops most of their working lives. So the closest we came to vacationing was a trip to the Dairy Queen or Snack Shack after a Friday night football game. They just did not travel much, mostly due to the fact that vacations meant spending money we did not have, and it would take them away from their work responsibilities.

We did manage to make it on a couple of short vacations. One was to the Astrodome when it first opened so that we could see the Yankees and Astros play an exhibition game and see the Eighth Wonder of the World (which is what the Astrodome was dubbed at the time). The other one I remember was also to the Houston area to visit the Battleship Texas and see the San Jacinto monument. Other than visiting San Antonio to see our relatives for Christmas and sometimes Easter and working in a trip to see the Alamo (which I was enamored with at the time), we just did not have vacations or leisure time. Such time for us was having homemade ice cream, hamburgers with the relatives, and sitting in our lawn chairs while we ate. That was about as leisure as we got as a family.

So this whole idea of "getting away for a while" has been rather foreign to me. It actually kind of blew my mind that a professor was teaching such a course and getting paid for it! But the conversation did get me to thinking, and I will write more about that later in this chapter. For now, I want to take a step back and write about work and leisure and the juxtaposition of the two.

WORK AND THE WORK ETHIC

So much about our lives would be at least a little easier to understand if we would begin at the beginning. Why do we have to work, why do some seem to have such a strong disdain for it, and why others thrive on it?

I began working my first job when I was eleven. Word got out that a paper route was coming open, and Dad made sure my name made it to the publisher. The kid previous to me on this route had, apparently, not bothered to collect each month, so his parents ended up shelling out about $80 a month to cover his expenses. They wisely decided that this was not going to continue, so he had to give up the route.

My dear dad sat me down and made something very clear to me. He said, "Son, you are doing this to learn something about work and to make some money. You will need to be responsible for collecting the money for the paper each month because your mom and I are not going to cover that expense for you." I was fairly bright and was already decent at math and could calculate amazingly quickly that I couldn't afford to cough up $80 each month that I did not have! (Oh, that our government would figure this out, but then they don't have a dad telling them that *he* is not covering the expense. But that's another book!) So the first Saturday morning of each month, rain or shine, I was on my red Western Flyer, with my money bag, covering my route to collect what people owed for the monthly bill for the paper. Amazing how this works: by collecting from everyone each month, I actually *made* $80 a month, and in 1966 for a kid, this was big money! And, of course, Dad was proud of me, which made me feel proud too.

What does this story have to do with leisure since this is what the chapter is supposed to be about?

We must get an understanding of work and where it started to get a better understanding of leisure and why it is necessary. And work, contrary to what many believe and hold dear, is not a blessing. *What?* Nope. Not a blessing. I know that this sounds heretical, but let's look from where this stems.

Remember I said just a few lines previous to this that we need to begin at the beginning. So that is what we will do.

The book of Genesis is such a wonderful book in so many ways, and one of the ways in which it teaches us so much is in what it teaches us about rest and work. *Genesis 2:2* tells us that "And He [God] *rested* on the seventh day from all His work which He had done." Now I am not here to debate whether or not this is a literal day or what "day" meant or to get into any of the arguments pro or con about any of this. So you will know, I take it at face value. The point is not to debate. The point is that the God of the universe—Omnipotent, Omniscient, holy, and glorious—worked like mad for six days and *rested* on the seventh. If the God who created the universe and all that is within its realm rested on the seventh day, it would seem that rest is kind of important for mere mortals such as you and me!

Genesis 3:17–19 gives us our first look at the curse, not the blessing, of what we call work. Here is the whole passage:

> Cursed is the ground because of you; In toil you
> shall eat of it all the days of your life. Both thorns
> and thistles it shall grow for you; And you shall

eat the plants of the field; *By the sweat of your face, you shall eat bread, till you return to the ground, because from it you were taken; For you are dust, and to dust you shall return.*

There is not one word in this passage about this being a blessing. Adam and Eve had the best of all worlds. Literally. God had provided their food; they had no work to do other than naming animals and enjoying both the food provided and the pleasure of the company of the first domesticated animals. All they had to do to continue in this paradise was stay away from one tree. Just one. Not two, not three, just one. The garden was loaded with all kinds of provision for them that they had never, or would they ever have to work to produce. Just stay away from that one tree.

And, of course, we know the end result of that, and we and all of nature are the products of what happened. But work became a burden, a curse. Food and other products would be produced by the sweat of our brows, and so we find ourselves today with this curse we call work. If we are going to have food, pay bills, be productive, create things such as computer I am typing on, then we will have to work. Bummer!

So as much as it pleased my dad and as much satisfaction as I derived out of making my own money at age eleven, it was still part of the curse of working.

I need to make it clear that by saying that work is a curse does not mean that we don't draw satisfaction out of a good day of work, or that work, in and of itself, is evil. Far from it. But, work was given as a punishment for a massive disobedience in the garden, and we still live with the effects today. That is all that is being said.

With the arrival of the pilgrims on what is now American soil, rules for communities were established, which evolved into what became known as the "Protestant work ethic." Work, itself, became an end unto itself and was looked upon as something very positive and desirable. And without it, nothing would get built, nothing would get accomplished, and progress would not move forward. So the Protestant work ethic became part of the warp and woof of society and carried over for centuries into what became our culture.

Such a work ethic has served us well. From that standpoint, the curse of work we inherited from Genesis turned into a positive. However, lost in the shuffle was the necessity of rest and leisure, and we became a nation obsessed with work. The onset of the industrial revolution in this country in the nineteenth century brought about the need for unions and child labor laws, for women and children were literally being worked to death. There was no such thing as a forty-hour workweek. The work day was long and hot and wearying to the body and soul.

Even in our own time, it is recorded that work dominates our lives. Al Gini, in his book *The Importance of Being Lazy* states, "From approximately the ages of 21 to 70, we will spend our lives working. We will not sleep as much, spend as much time with our families, eat as much, or recreate and rest as much as we will work" (pg. 8).

He goes on to say this: "America has always been a land and a society of contrasts and paradoxes. One of the most glaring conflicts in our constellation of cultural values is our duplicitous attitude in regard to the Protestant work ethic. On the one hand, we have always praised work… On the other hand, let's be frank, we also think that work stinks!… And given the option, a lot of us would gladly never work again" (pg. 8–9).

THE ENTITLEMENT MENTALITY

The dilemma that we confront on almost a daily basis is the stark contrast between working to find purpose and to be productive (even if he is correct in stating that a lot of us would gladly never work again, and I believe he is correct. I'm certainly right there with him!) and not working and expecting government to provide for us from cradle to grave.

There are a plethora of consequences, which came out of the Great Depression of the 1930s, but one of those has been the entitlement mentality that has developed in this country. Two developments in the early part of the twentieth century in this country have helped to bring about this mentality. One was the passing of the Sixteenth Amendment. This created the income tax and, worse yet, the IRS. The second such significant development was the passing of legislation under FDR to create Social Security. What was intended for good has turned into an entitlement vehicle, and one which has helped to create a mentality that says, "You owe me." And with the creation of that Frankenstein we call the IRS, the government created the means to collect from we, the people, in order to have the funds to distribute at the discretion (if one may call it that) of Congress.

Dr. Marvin Olasky has written an important book on the subject of welfare and social policy entitled *The Tragedy of American Compassion*. While there is much more to his book than what I will say here, his book points out how much changed in the twentieth century with socialist type of government programs taking over the jobs that churches were doing in the nineteenth century. Churches were always compassionate but would not allow people who could work to develop a mental attitude which expected, and in many cases demanded, they be taken care of. Churches would work with people to help those in need find work but would not allow them to continue to be slothful, if indeed that was the case. In our time, the Salvation Army continues to practice this same type of ministry.

So in a chapter dealing with rest and relaxation, what does this have to do with the topic?

It deals with the ongoing dilemma we face in contrasting work with leisure and in contrasting work and slothfulness. Those who really like to work tend to feel guilty for taking time off for rest and relaxation and tend to think that such rest is being slothful. On the other hand, those who are more than happy for the government or some other agency to keep them up see work differently and would like nothing better than to be on permanent vacation. So what we are looking for here is the balance that is needed in understanding both work and rest.

LEISURE AND REST

As I have pondered this chapter in the book, I have considered why such a chapter would even be written in a book that is supposed to be a "basic primer" of Christian theology. *How*, I have thought, *does something like this belong in the book?*

Well, first of all, it came from the title of the song. It was the title that got me thinking about how little we deal with how we practice the faith when it comes to rest and leisure. In fact, there may be books out there that deal with it, but I am not sure I have seen them. Second, I realized that what made the ministry of Jesus so powerfully effective was the fact that he took time away from people to pray and meditate and speak with the Father. (See Mark 6:31–32, Mark 6:46, John 8:1, Matthew 8:1, 13:1, 14:13, 23).

Having said this, there is the danger of going to an extreme when it comes to vacationing and resting and having a life of leisure. People will say, "Well, I think I will get away for a while," meaning they are checking out for about six months! Since the ministry of Jesus was about three years, taking six months would have been a little on the imbalanced side. I can see Him saying to the disciples, "Hey, guys, I am a little weary. Been casting out demons, healing the sick, preaching, teaching, dealing with the Pharisees and Sadducees, and walking quite a bit, so I am going to rest and relax for the next six months!" Right. *That* would have worked.

Again, balance is what we should be striving for. Work, the curse that it is, is still necessary and ultimately meaningful, while rest and leisure helps us to refocus and to reenergize.

As I spoke to the professor on the plane, I asked her what were some of the things she found about our patterns? She mentioned that there were certain places, such as Florida and Colorado, that tended to see more than their share of those seeking rest and relaxation, and of course, Hawaii. Cruises in the Bahamas and Alaska also made the list of prominent getaways. Since I had lived in Oregon, I asked her about the Northwest. Of course, she had been there on "research" (there's that word again) and found that in many ways, it was kind of an untapped oasis of beauty, but that people were beginning to discover this untapped reservoir of natural outdoor beauty. I suggested that maybe all of the rain kept people away, and she said that was a factor, but more important was the relative unknown about the Northwest itself.

More important to me than all else, I wondered about whether or not we, as Americans, didn't vacate too much anyway. Surprisingly, she responded that research had indicated just the opposite. We work too much. It was then that she suggested I purchase the book *The Importance of Being Lazy*, which I have quoted from in this chapter. It was a very interesting conversation and a very important one for me.

It got me thinking about what we do as Christians and was there a place for balance in all of this? And biblically, was there some kind of teaching that was missing on this topic? The Bible speaks of "rest," but it is used more often than not as a reference to "entering into His rest," which is not quite the same thing as having a retreat or just taking a rest and relaxation tour. The psalmist in *Psalm 37:7* says, "Rest in the Lord, and wait patiently for Him." *Jeremiah 6:16* says, "Stand by the ways, and see and ask for the ancient paths, Where the good way is, and walk in it; And you shall find rest for your souls."

Jesus says in *Matthew 11:28*, "Come to Me, all who are weary and heavy-laden, and I will give you rest."

The example we should look to is the example that Jesus set when he would sit by the sea, go up into the mountains, or get out on a boat in the water by Himself just to get away for a bit to be by Himself. From my childhood, there has perhaps been nothing more relaxing or resting for me than to be outside at night on a perfectly clear night and talk with God as I admire the stars He created as they twinkle in the sky. I don't sit and ponder the vastness of time and space and wonder about galaxies I see and don't see and contemplate the mass and matter and gases of each planet and star that I see, or do I consider all of the math and science that is involved in calculating the speed of light or in trying to understand the stars and the universe, which encompasses those stars. No, I just get to relax and talk with God as I simply soak in the beauty that I see on a starry, starry night.

Beyond this, however, are times in each of our lives when we just need to rest and relax. That will mean different things for different people. To some, it will mean hitting the beach. To others, it will mean heading for the mountains. To others, it will mean visiting relatives (though I am not always sure how relaxing that might be). And to yet others, it will mean just taking off from work and doing absolutely nothing but reading a good book, listening to good music, or doing not one thing you don't want to do.

For others, taking a vacation and actually going somewhere might be the ticket. Vacations can be tricky. I have found that some vacations I have taken were ones which were so anxiety-filled that going back to work was actually less work than the vacation! But the bottom line is to do whatever floats your boat that will relieve some stress, help you to refill the tank, and refocus whatever it is you need to be focused on. As the title of the song says, let's go away for a while!

CHAPTER 7

Sloop John B

"The things I thought were so important—because of the effort I put into them—have turned out to be of small value. And the things I never thought about, the things I was never able either to measure or to expect, were the things that mattered."

—Thomas Merton

"Christians cherish a mythology that, along with their theology, shapes and directs their lives. Perhaps no myth more strongly influences us than our understanding of how to know the will of God... If we ask, 'How can I know the will of God?' we may be asking the wrong question... Instead of wondering, 'How do I find the will of God?' a better question to pursue is, 'How do I make good decisions?'"

—Haddon Robinson

"This is the worst trip I've ever been on."
—Brian Wilson in "Sloop John B"

"Where there is no command, God gives us freedom (and responsibility) to choose… With freedom comes relief that I am not missing God's will. At the same time, being responsible for my decisions means that I cannot blame bad decisions on God."
—Gary Friesen

"Lying behind every myth concerning God's will is a myth about God."
—Kyle Lake

When I was a young boy, one of the delights I was privileged to enjoy was celebrating Easter with a yearly Easter egg hunt. Even in understanding later in life that much of what and how we celebrate Easter draws upon pagan rituals tied into fertility rites, and incorporating the Easter bunny into the ritual was part of this celebration, nonetheless, I have fairly fond memories of hunting for the hidden ovals of sugary delight. Usually, my parents and my aunt would "hide" the eggs, and my cousin and I would thrill to loading up our Easter baskets with as many eggs as we could find. Early on, I learned to loathe the hard-boiled eggs even though they were decorated in a fine assortment of colors. I just didn't like hard-boiled eggs! And I preferred the candy eggs that were wrapped in the individual wrappers. They always seemed to be fresher than those that weren't wrapped for some reason.

What is important to know is that my parents and my aunt actually hid the eggs and didn't just throw them out on the ground for us to collect. What fun would that have been? If it rained, the hunt took place inside, but if it was dry that day, there was nothing like being outside looking in bushes, trees, porch chairs, and other hidden nooks where the eggs had been placed. When my own children were little, I duplicated this ritual for them, and they had such fun gathering the eggs into the baskets. The only difference was that, by the time they had come along, plastic eggs had been created, and we would put coins in some of those rather than candy or sugary eggs so that they would have something other than just sugar poisoning their bodies!

The traditional approach to finding the will of God has been rather like those Easter egg hunts. We have been taught that one must pray for and find the perfect will of God for our lives, in much the same way that parents hide Easter eggs and tell their kids to find them. The eggs, like the will of God, remain hidden until we stumble upon them. And so we have been taught.

In dealing with Christian thought and Christianity itself, sooner or later, the issue of "how do I find the will of God?" is going to demand attention. It is unfair, in one sense, to limit writing about the topic of the will of God to one chapter, for books have been written that are very broad in scope and that cover the topic much more clearly than one chapter will allow. However, if we are going to deal with a broad view of Christian living, it is also unfair to leave this topic completely out of the discussion. My hope is to encourage you to further study this topic beyond what we will cover here and to leave you with a deeper appetite for pursuing this further.

It is a subject I have struggled with mightily through the years, for the tendency is to always go back to what I thought was correct, be it a fleece set out before God so that I would "know" what His will was or to look for some sign that would surely point me in the way I needed to go. Such was the way that I would approach which school to attend, which girl to date, which one was "the one", which car to buy, which job to take, and on and on like this. Unfortunately, approaching the will of God this way doesn't tend to work out very well, and you end up always questioning if you "really heard God" on that one, or did I somehow "mess up" and not hear Him clearly. When things don't seem to work out as one thinks they are supposed to, doubt about hearing God clearly always works its way into the equation, even to the point of trying to blame God for the decision made, as if He led me astray.

As some of you are reading this, you are identifying with exactly what I am saying. We will get into this more in depth as we move along, but when dealing with the will of God, our tendency is to focus on the *individual will*, and as one author has stated, trying to land in the middle of the "dot" for our lives. And this is exactly where each of us gets thrown off course, for we have been taught and believed a lie about finding this elusive "individual will." So hang on as we sail the murky waters of seeking to know the will of God and see if we are asking the right questions in the first place!

WHAT IS THE WILL OF GOD?

How often in the Bible do we read that Jesus said we are to "do the will of the Father?" It is there numerous times, yet the big question that arises from this command is, "Just what is the will of God?" Any of us who have been serious about wanting to follow God's will have asked this question on more than one occasion and on more than one occasion have wondered why we don't seem to get any sort of answer. A letter would be helpful, or maybe a thunderbolt at just the right time, or some other "sign" that would be "the sign" that we were looking for, even though we really weren't sure what that was supposed to be. And then, there are those who "hear" God speak to them so clearly that one has to wonder why we don't hear quite so well when we are trying to listen, too. What, we ask, is wrong with us that we don't seem to hear as clearly? Are we just not spiritual enough? Are we not praying hard enough? Is there something amiss in our spiritual lives that causes us to become deaf when wanting to hear the voice of God? Just what is the problem that causes us to miss out on this perfect will of God for our lives?

Well, maybe, just maybe, we are asking the wrong questions. Let's look at some of the traditional ways we have been taught to find the will of God.

Traditional Views. First, one of the ways seems to be very biblical because it draws its teaching directly from the Bible. It is in the Bible, so shouldn't it be a "biblical principle for finding the will of God?" It is known as "laying out a *fleece.*" It comes from Judges 6:36–40 and is the story of Gideon. In Judges 6:11–24, Gideon had already asked for a "sign" regarding who it was that was speaking to him. With this sign confirmed, we come later in the chapter to the following:

> Then Gideon said to God, "If Thou wilt deliver Israel through me, as Thou hast spoken, behold, I will put a *fleece* of wool on the threshing floor. If there is dew on the fleece only, and it is dry on all the ground, then I will know that Thou wilt deliver Israel through me, as Thou hast spoken." And it was so. When he arose early the next morning and squeezed the fleece, he drained the dew from the fleece, a bowl full of water. Then Gideon said to God, "Do not let Thine anger burn against me that I may speak once more; please let me make a test once more with the fleece, let it now be dry only on the fleece, and let there be dew on all the ground." And God did so that night; for it was dry only on the fleece, and dew was on all the ground.

Now if we are honest with one another, most, if not all, of us have used this method somewhere along the way in our Christian lives. If Gideon did it and it's in the Bible, then shouldn't that be good enough for us? This is one of the methods used in dating when we are or were young. It is tied into the phone call, and the fleece we laid out was in the manner of how the phone call wasn't answered the first time, and if she didn't answer a second call, then it was obviously God's will for there to be no connection. If the line was busy, then that, too, meant not to call again, for she was probably on the phone with some other guy. The "fleece" method could be used for just about anything so that, ultimately, I was not responsible for the final choice made but could lay the end result at God's feet. It takes real decision making out of our hands and allows us to place the responsibility for the outcome on God.

Some will argue with this and say that because Gideon did it, then we can, too, and that it should be a valid method of finding God's will. Notice, however, that Gideon's first answer wasn't enough for him. No, he laid out a second fleece before God. As much as we would all like to be able to constantly lay out fleeces to find an answer, it is really not a biblical norm for finding the will of God. In fact, the story of Gideon is the only time we see this particular way of approaching God's will in all of the Bible. And, it is told as part of a story, not as a biblical principle.

The truth is there have been times that this method has seemed to work for us, hasn't it? As often as not, however, what so often happens is that we bring several fleeces before God until we get the answer we have *really* been wanting to hear. We're just not sure if God got our first fleece request right, and we want to give Him a second and sometimes third chance to make sure He heard us correctly. Could it be that the method is flawed and not the recipient of the fleece request?

A second way we have been led to believe is correct is the method of "impressions." This can come in the form of signs or inner impressions. Dr. Gary Friesen, in his excellent book *Decision Making and the Will of God* lays it out as follows:

"The Traditional View of Decision Making"

Premise: For each of our decisions, God has a perfect plan or will.

Purpose: The goal of the believer is to discover God's individual will (find the dot) and make decisions in accordance with it.

Process: The believer interprets inner impressions and outward signs, which the Holy Spirit uses to communicate God's individual will.

Proof: The confirmation that one has correctly discerned the individual will of God comes from an inner sense of peace and outward (successful) results of the decision. (Friesen, *Decision Making and the Will of God*, pg. 110)

Such impressions or such inner peace is very subjective and can turn on us at any time. What gave us peace yesterday completely frightens us tomorrow, and the surety we had that we had found the elusive and perfect "will of God" for our individual lives is lost in this sea of subjectivity.

I worked for a time as claims adjuster for an insurance company. One of the many interesting aspects of that job was getting a clear description of what happened during a car wreck. It was always rather fascinating to be looking at the same accident as the people involved and getting completely different stories as to what happened. Trying to gain as much objectivity as possible entailed getting a police report, recorded statements from those involved, pictures of the autos involved, photos of the skid marks, and any statements from witnesses who might have seen what happened. The subjectivity involved from the participants was part of the challenge of determining what actually occurred. And I found out that many people just found it easier to not tell the truth, not realizing that eventually, we would get to what in actuality was the truth.

The subjectivity and the particular view of the situation of the participants is similar in nature to what "inner impressions" and "signs" can be for the believer who relies on those to determine what the individual will of God is for their lives. How do we know that the inner impression we have isn't last night's pizza or ice cream? And how many times have we relied on such impressions, made decisions, and then discovered that our feelings were what really dictated the impression we had from God. We want to appear to be spiritual and what better way than giving the appearance of having "just a closer walk with Thee." It can be a very dangerous, slippery slope.

This is not to say that God cannot or will not, at times, clearly be giving a person direction in making a decision. He is God and will do what He will, and that will sometimes involve being very clear in His direction for someone. It is not, however, the norm.

Let me illustrate. When God spoke to Solomon and told him to ask for anything he wanted, Solomon's response was to ask for wisdom. God granted this request immediately, and Solomon became known as the wisest person who ever lived. This was clear and personal. I have never met, read about, or heard of any other person who received wisdom in this manner. Every person who has asked for wisdom from God may have been given wisdom in a one-time circumstance, but wisdom comes from God from asking and receiving it over a lifetime of experiences and living for the rest of us. I have never seen an exception to this, even though I have met some very wise Christian people. Unlike Solomon, they didn't get the wisdom overnight.

Several years ago, Campus Crusade for Christ had a very aggressive approach to evangelism on college campuses. Part of their strategy involved having students knock on dormitory doors, with the hope of finding someone on the other side of that door who perhaps was not a Christian and with whom they could share their "Four Spiritual Laws" booklet. It began with the phrase, "God has a wonderful plan for your life." I have a great deal of respect for the ministry of Campus Crusade for Christ and met some truly dedicated young men and women involved with their ministry. I had a bit of a problem with their methodology, however. I was one of the ones who had their door knocked on, and the presentation put me off. The person at my door had no idea who I was, we had no relationship, and I was being told that "God has a wonderful plan for your life." *How*, I thought, *would this guy know?* And if so, what, exactly, was this wonderful plan? In its own way, this was one form of having someone believe that God had a *specific* plan for my life, and all I had to do was to just ask. With such asking, I could know the perfect will of God for my life.

The intentions were certainly good and noble, but had I followed this line of thinking to its conclusion, I would then assume that there was a perfect, specific will of God for my life, and I simply had to find it. Once found, I could move forward with my life, and this perfect plan would just unfold before me as I marched on through life. Pretty easy, huh? Oh, that it would be that simple.

But so much of what we have been taught about the will of God centers around this perfect, individual will for a person's life, if we will only listen to the Holy Spirit and lay out our fleeces and search for signs and impressions that we are on the right path. In doing so, we will find peace and direction and will always know that we are in the dead center of God's will for our lives. Right? Except that we are really asking the wrong questions and spending a good part of our lives frustrated and always wondering if we are on the right or wrong path. And, if we are not careful, we come to understand that the words in "Sloop John B" become prophetic of our trip through life. "This is the worst trip I've ever been on."

What then can we discover about the will of God, and how do we go about attempting to make wise decisions?

WHAT WE KNOW ABOUT THE WILL OF GOD

The Psalmist writes in Psalm 40:8, "I delight to do Thy will, O my God; Thy Law is within my heart." Paul writes to the church at Ephesus in Ephesians 5:17, "So then do not be foolish, but understand what the will of the Lord is." Romans 12:2 says, "And do not be conformed to this world, but be transformed by the renewing of your mind, that you may prove *what the will of God is,* that which is good and acceptable and perfect." So what then do we know about "what the will of the Lord is?"

Before answering that question, we should start where Scripture starts, and that is by telling us that in order to understand and prove what the will of God is, we must be disciples of His word. There is no shortcut, there is no way around this, there are no "Cliff Notes" to getting in on this thing we call the will of God. He has given us His Word in the form of the sacred Scriptures, and in order to know some (and I would add, most) of what His will is in the world, we must know what the Bible says. And in order for that to happen, we in Western culture need to shake the dust off our Bibles, open them, and read and study them. This is where we begin. First Corinthians 2:11 reminds us why this is crucial to our understanding: "For who among men knows the thoughts of a man except the spirit of the man, which is in him? Even so the thoughts of God no one knows except the Spirit of God."

This does not say that men don't understand women, or that women don't understand men. This is not a Mars-Venus thing. No, it goes far beyond that and says that *no one* knows the thoughts of another person except the spirit that is in that person. The story is told of a man who is praying, and the Lord speaks to him from heaven and says, "I hear you. What can I do for you?" The man replies that he has never been to Hawaii and would like to go, but he doesn't like flying and will not get on a ship or a boat, so he would like for the Lord to build a long bridge from California to Hawaii so that he can make the drive in his car. The Lord says to the man, "Do you realize how deep the ocean is, how far it is from the coast of California to Hawaii, and just how much steel and concrete and other materials that it would take to build such a bridge? Pick something else." So the man says, "Well, okay, Lord, I would like to understand women." The Lord replies, "Will that be a two-lane or a four-lane highway?"

The point is that we don't even know our own hearts and minds, much less anyone else's, and certainly not God's. Thus, in order to know some of the "thoughts of God," we must be reading and studying that which He gave us in order to know Him, and that is His Word.

So then, back to the original question: what do we know about what the will of the Lord is?

Dr. Gary Friesen says that "the traditional view of God's will may be understood in three ways: God's *sovereign will*, His *moral will*, and His *individual will*." He goes on to say that "the Bible clearly teaches that God has a sovereign will, a 'secret plan for everything that happens in the universe'" (Friesen, *Decision Making and the Will of God*, pg. 40).

I have been asked on several occasions, what does *sovereign* mean? When I was a youth pastor many years ago, I would often pray and thank God for His "sovereignty" in our lives. A student finally asked me one day what exactly did I mean when I thanked Him for being sovereign. I told him that the easiest way to think of this is that God is in complete control of this world, and He has rule over it at all times. Nothing escapes Him. Just as a king was sovereign over his kingdom, (meaning he had control over all his subjects and all of that which was a part of this kingdom), so the Lord is in ultimate control over all of creation.

Friesen says further, "The Scriptures clearly reveal all of the moral will of God" (pg. 41). "It is fully conveyed," says Friesen, "in the Bible and so does not have to 'found' –just read, learned, and obeyed" (pg. 15). We could begin with something very basic to most moral and ethical laws that have been written, and that is the Ten Commandments. We can know for certain that we are not to kill, steal, commit adultery, and covet people or possessions. These are the moral laws we know for certain. This is a great start. Paul tells us in 1 Corinthians 6:18 to "Flee immorality. Every other sin that a man commits is outside the body, but the immoral man sins against his own body." So knowing there is a moral will of God, we can be fairly assured that fleeing immorality would fall under His will.

So what we know so far is that God has a sovereign will and a moral will. This, you may be saying, is great to know, but what about knowing very specifically what is His will for and in my life? How can I know the will of God for my life?

ASKING THE WRONG QUESTION

Because I tend to be rather stubborn, rather than learning this when I was much younger, it has taken me a good part of four decades to learn that we have been asking the wrong question when it comes to wanting to know the will of God for our lives. What we should be asking is how do I go about making wise decisions within the sovereign and moral boundaries that God *has* clearly revealed in His word? In other words, how do I make good decisions?

I have known of Christians who were so determined to not miss God's will in any aspect of their lives that they would pray to determine what socks to wear, what pants or skirts to wear, what blouse or shirt or what tie, etc. *ad nauseam ad infinitum.* I have great news! God does not really care what you wear; just wear something that is appropriate for the occasion! You have that wonderful freedom to choose!

As we go about discovering how to make good, wise decisions, we have to understand something that Kyle Lake wrote about in his book *Understanding God's Will.* He wrote very wisely, "So, herein lies a major misconception about God's will – namely, that *God's will is the path of least resistance.* It seems as though the predominant Christian creed that governs our approach to God's will is: If we are truly following God, things will just pan out… our road will become much smoother… and with God on our side, we'll not encounter near as many obstacles in life as other people do." He writes earlier that "The Gospel narratives in the New Testament reveal that a life lived in close proximity to Jesus is not bland, usual, or ordinary. Quite the contrary. Anyone who chooses this life can expect an amazing adventure-one that involves hazards, risk, and unknowns" (Kyle Lake, *Understanding God's Will,* pg. 38–39). What makes this passage more poignant is that, not long after it was written, this young pastor was electrocuted in a freak baptismal accident that sadly took his life. Unknowns, indeed.

I relate all too clearly with what he wrote. There is a tendency to think and believe that, if I am in God's will, the road will rise up to meet me, all will be roses, and the path will be perfectly clear, and life will just be one victory piled upon another. As we see from a clear study of Scripture, nothing could be further from the truth. Being in His will may cost us our earthly lives. What does that do to your view of such decision making and "understanding" what the will of God is?

I want to be clear that there are a number of Christian thinkers, theologians, pastors, and authors who have varying views of what the "will of God" is for an individual, and those views vary in as many ways as there are books and articles written on the subject. It is not an easy subject with which to deal because knowing and doing the will of God is such a highly debated and highly personal subject. The question needing to be asked, however, is important, and that is, How do I make wise, good, godly decisions?

I DIDN'T SEE THAT COMING

Earlier, I wrote about Solomon and the fact that he had a chance to ask God for anything and asked for wisdom. He writes in Proverbs 1:5, "A wise man will hear and increase in learning. And a man of *understanding* will acquire wise counsel." In Proverbs 3:13, he writes, "How blessed is the man who finds wisdom. And the man who gains *understanding*." Proverbs 4:1 tells us, "Hear, O sons, the instruction of a father, and give attention that you may gain *understanding*." Proverbs 11:14 says, "Where there is no guidance, the people fall. But in abundance of counselors there is deliverance." Proverbs 12:15 tells us, "The way of a fool is right in his own eyes, but a wise man is he who listens to counsel." Solomon, the man to whom God gave wisdom and whom we are informed became the wisest man who ever lived, says more about seeking counsel than *any other author in the Old and New Testaments*. Why do you think that is?

I am going to borrow from a sermon I heard Andy Stanley give in a series he did entitled, "Ask." Have you ever said to yourself, "Well, I just didn't see that coming"? Why is it that I could see it coming to or at you, but you couldn't see it coming? And why is it that you could see it coming to or at me, but I couldn't see it coming?

We all have natural blinders on when it comes to making decisions without seeking counsel, and things happen that we just did not see coming, but somebody else saw it as plain as day.

How do we go about making good decisions for ourselves? If we will hear the wisest man who ever lived, we can begin by seeking wise counsel from those who do not have our set of natural blinders on and who can give us good counsel. How much grief I could have spared myself if I had taken this teaching to heart in so many decisions made over the years because, on my own, I could not see it coming. I could not see what some decisions would produce as a consequence in my life. And I would venture to say that some of you reading this can say the same thing.

The age-old problem that we must all deal with is the problem of pride. We all want to think that we can do it on our own, that we are the smartest people in the room, that it is manly or womanly to figure it out by ourselves. Human pride can lead us into making really foolish decisions that have bad consequences on down the road.

However, to "understand and prove" what the will of God is, seeking wise counsel is not only necessary; it is mandatory. If Solomon said more about this than anyone, perhaps it would be wise to hear what he had to say about an "abundance of counselors." In numbers, there is a certain amount of safety.

IN SUMMARY

So to tie this chapter into a nice, neat package, let me summarize what this very short chapter on knowing the will of God has to say.

First of all, we can say that the will of God can be divided into three separate components: (1) His sovereign will – His overall plan for the world and mankind (2) His moral will – those things that the Bible tells us we are to read, learn, and obey. (3) The Way of Wisdom.

Quoting Dr. Friesen, he says that, "God's guidance according to the way of wisdom can be summarized in four simple statements:

1.   Where God commands, we must obey.
2.   Where there is no command, God gives freedom (and responsibility) to choose.
3.   Where there is no command, God gives us wisdom to choose.
4.   When we have chosen what is moral and wise, we must trust the sovereign God to work all the details together for good."

Second, when it comes to knowing about the will of God in my life, it needs to be made clear that there exists in the mind of God a perfect plan or will for each of our lives, but since we are finite and are not God, knowing this perfect plan is probably not a foregone conclusion. Therefore, we are to call upon three resources to go about "understanding and proving" what the will of God is, and those three resources are:

1.   The Bible – we are to read, learn, and obey in those things that are made clear in His Word.
2.   Seek Counsel – to help avoid those blind spots, seeking counsel from others before making life altering decisions is mandatory.
3.   Prayer – certainly, there are going to be times when God has made it abundantly clear through personal prayer what is His will for us and we must be in prayer in order to know what this is."

As I said earlier, it is impossible to do justice to the topic of knowing the will of God in one small chapter, but what I have written may be used to both help clarify some things and to encourage you to do further study in regards to learning more about God's will. It is a never-ending learning process, and it is also a never-ending battle.

On a personal note, I can tell you that there have been times in my life when I have either forgotten or refused to go by the principles I have mentioned, and I have always paid the price. I have prayed to the point of buckets of tears, hoping to hear a clear voice from heaven in regards to direction in life, and so many times, I seemed to be greeted with silence. That is because, though God will speak to you and me clearly at times, those times are not the norm because He has laid out principles to follow. For example, if Solomon puts such great emphasis on seeking godly counsel, then it seems to be prudent that I would do just that and seek out such counsel. Unfortunately, I have not always done that.

One of the best pieces of advice I ever heard was to simply do or obey the will of God in those areas where it is crystal clear and where you know beyond a shadow of a doubt what you are to do, and the rest becomes easier. Not easy, but easier. Just do what you know to do, and then you or I will have to speak the words about life from the song, "Sloop John B": "This is the worst trip I've ever been on!" In fact, quite the opposite will be true.

CHAPTER 8

God Only Knows

"In the beginning, God created the heavens and the earth."

—Genesis 1:1

"O Lord, Thou hast searched me and known me. Thou dost know when I sit down and when I rise up... Even before there is a word on my tongue, Behold, O Lord, Thou dost know it all... Such knowledge is too wonderful for me. It is too high, I cannot attain to it."

—Psalm 139:1–2, 4, 6

"One can know a great deal about God without much knowledge of Him."

—J. I. Packer, *Knowing God*, pg. 21

"Let not a wise man boast of his wisdom, and let not the mighty man boast of his might, let not a rich man boast of his riches; but let him

who boasts boast of this, that he understands and
knows Me, that I am the Lord who exercises lov-
ingkindness, justice, and righteousness on earth;
for I delight in these things, declares the Lord."
—Jeremiah 9:23–24

"Men are never duly touched and impressed with
a conviction of their insignificance until they
have contrasted themselves with the majesty of
God."
—John Calvin

"Too much of our time is spent trying to chart
God on a grid, and too little is spent allowing our
hearts to feel awe."
—Donald Miller

There is no other subject, no other topic, no other person whom
one can write about who can give you the feeling of extraordinary
smallness than writing about the knowledge of God. In mathemat-
ical terms, it is the finite trying to get some semblance of a grip on
He who is infinite. How does one understand and know God? Even
more complicated, how does one tell others about this God we are to
understand and know, and then even boast about it?

I have alluded to this previously, but I want to elaborate on
something I mentioned earlier in another chapter. When I was a kid,
my first real awareness of knowing that there was something much
bigger than me in the universe was when I would go outside on a
clear night and either sit on the trunk of the car or sit in a lawn chair
in our front yard and be astonished at the vastness of the stars and
of the universe. I have always seemed to have had a keen awareness
of God's presence in my life, long before I was saved and was given a

much clearer understanding of God's grace and just what it was He did with His Son, Jesus, on the cross. I would sit gazing upward and just talk with God, sometimes out loud. I told Him everything my little mind could think of and just imagined Him listening to every word as if what I was saying was breathtaking and news to Him. I was pretty much an only child (my half-sister was twelve years older than me and was already gone by the time I had a halfway semi-conscious thought!), so these times on the back of the car are some of the most cherished memories I have of talking to God. He was kind of like having a "big brother," only much bigger! It was before life got complicated, and our "chats" were really simple. I just talked about whatever was on my mind, be it baseball, piano lessons, swimming, that cute little girl I had a secret crush on, things troubling my mom and dad, or what I really would like to have for Christmas.

Sometimes, I would just sit in silence for a long time and absorb whatever it was He was wanting me to absorb. Life wasn't so complex, and my mind wasn't so cluttered, and I could sit for what seemed like hours and just simply enjoy His company as if I was the only person in the universe. What always amazed me was knowing that He was having the same type of visits and conversations with other kids sitting on the back of their cars wherever they might be, but I never felt the least bit neglected or slighted. I instinctively knew that they didn't either.

As I think about those nights, I cannot help but think that the simplicity of that relationship is really how it is supposed to be. Yet I also know that an infinite being is much more deep and complex than what a young boy can fathom, and that God's characteristics go far beyond those kind, simple talks we had on clear nights.

Even as I write these words, I am keenly aware that not all children had the privilege of having those nights on the back of a car. Some children had (and have) to be strong simply to survive. There was little food and certainly no car to sit on to have those chats.

Many lived, and live, in conditions that I cannot fathom, and probably have different kinds of prayers than what I had. While I was fortunate to have a great earthly father, many either don't have a father or have a father who instills the wrong kind of fear in them, for these children fear and have a mental picture of a father who beats them without cause or who left when they were very young. I remember talking with a young man once who told me that calling God "Heavenly Father" was almost impossible for him because of the horrible mental picture he had of a "father." So the God that the Bible describes for us is a foreign idea for some, but is truly an accurate description of the God who loves and cares for us in all of the beauty and ugliness that we encounter in this world.

THE GOD WHO IS THERE

One relatively small chapter on the person of God is not near enough to cover such a vast subject. How can one such chapter do justice to Him who is infinite? In reality, it cannot, but we can at least get a glimpse of who God is and something of His character.

One of the first Bible teachers I had taught about the character of God in the manner in which she had learned it and passed that knowledge on to several of us in the living room of her home. While the knowledge that was shared with us was true (God is Truth, Righteousness, Holy, Love, Mercy, Just, Omnipotent, Omniscient, Omnipresent), it tended to put God in a box. He is all of these things, but He is much more than the box of knowledge. This God eventually became a legalistic God, who could act only within the confines of the box. What happens, I wondered, when He makes a donkey talk? What happens when He commands a prophet to marry a known prostitute? What happens when He operates outside of the box? He does and will operate outside of the box precisely because He is God, and while He will not act inconsistently with His character, He is not limited to what we know of Him. Again, He is infinite, I am not.

In writing about knowing God, we must begin at the beginning. We begin with the assumption that God exists. *Genesis 1:1* says, "In the beginning, God created the heavens and the earth." *Hebrews 11:6* says, "And without faith it is impossible to please Him, for he who comes to God must believe that He is, and that He is a rewarder of those who seek Him." *John 1:1–2* begins much like Genesis 1:1 and says, "In the beginning was the Word, and the Word was with God, and the Word was God. He was in the beginning with God." As Francis Schaeffer once wrote, "We must never forget that the first part of the Gospel is not 'Accept Christ as Savior', but 'God is there.' Only then are we ready to hear God's solution for man's moral dilemma in the substitutionary work of Christ in history" (Schaeffer, Francis, *The God Who Is There*, pg. 132, IVP). So though it sounds almost redundant to say it this way, if we are to have true knowledge of God, we begin with simply believing that He is there.

It is important that this is the groundwork that must be laid, for we live at a time that our western culture is more relativistic than ever and more books on atheism have been written in the past five years than I can remember in my fifty plus years previous. What cannot be denied is that both positions (theism and atheism) ultimately come down to faith. And to know God, we must, as Hebrews says, "believe that He is."

DEEP THEOLOGICAL CONCEPTS

A look and study of God and who He is cannot be done without discussing some of the concepts of God that the world of theology would lead us to believe are absolutely crucial. In this world, God is studied under the heading of "Theology Proper" in which systematic theology lays out terms, which are probably useful in the world of theology but do not convey a great deal to most of us about who God actually *is*. While I don't want to be too cynical about this, for some of what theology teaches us is actually useful, dissecting God in this manner doesn't ultimately prove to be palpable for most of us.

When I was in seminary, one of the projects I was directed to write was a thirteen-week course on "Trinitarian Theism." It was a fairly useful exercise for me and was touted as a quarterly study that could be used for Sunday School or a thirteen week Bible study. I actually enjoyed doing the work and learned some things I would probably never have learned otherwise. So personally, there was some value in writing the course.

That was done some thirty years ago, and I have yet to use that study in any class or in any weekly Bible study. Why? Simply because most of the study was done as an academic exercise, using terms such as Trinitarian Theism, which convey a great theological concept of the Triune God, but do little to convey much about a truly personal God who loves us, calls us to be holy as He is holy, and commands us to forgive others as He has forgiven us.

The first time I used this term Trinitarian Theism with someone, I got a look I recognized very well. It was the same look I gave a guy the first time I heard him use the phrase "philosophical presuppositions." I came to learn what this meant, but initially, I was at a loss. Now one may think that others need to learn these terms, and that they can learn these terms, and there is certainly nothing wrong with that. But in reality, what does this convey about God other than that we can discuss theological terms about Him? As J. I. Packer has said, we can know a lot about God without actually knowing God. Big difference.

Another nineteenth century theologian, William G. T. Shedd, spoke of God in terms of "opera ad intra" and "opera ad extra." At the time of doing my course in Theology Proper, I was pretty impressed with such language and the depth of knowledge of God it seemed to convey. I have no doubt that Dr. Shedd had a deep personal knowledge of God. Again, however, such terminology seemed to communicate only with other theologians and those who studied theology for a living. What all of us have deep inside, whether we admit it or not, is not so much a desire for a theological knowledge of God but a knowledge that fills the "God-shaped" vacuum that Augustine referred to that is within each of us. We want to know this God who created the universe and all that is within it, and that we ultimately matter to Him.

Before too many conclusions are reached at this point, let me convey clearly that I am not being anti-intellectual and saying that we just need to know God with only our heart and at the emotional level. There is certainly some value in the study of God in theological terms. But for most of us, this type of knowledge doesn't serve to fill the void that is within us. If the Judeo-Christian God that we as Christians say we worship is personal, then what we need to know about God are the personal things about Him.

THE PERSONAL NATURE OF GOD

What is one major thing that distinguishes one person from another? Some may say looks, others may say intellect, still others may say hair color (assuming the color is the actual color!) or other such distinguishing features. But what sets us off as different from one another is personality. We may have some similarities in expressions, humor, seriousness, etc., but each of us has been given our own unique personality. If we were all alike, how boring would that be?

Where does personality originate, and how is it that we have personal relationships? Humanists would say we are just atoms thrown together randomly and just turn out that way. That there is no such "originating." Atheists would agree and would say we ultimately become food for worms, so personality doesn't matter nor does it originate from any source. We just are and are alone in the universe.

The title of the song that informs this chapter "God Only Knows," actually says something quite profound about the nature of God and His personality. Though the song is saying "God only knows what I'd be without you," kind of like a catch phrase we use, I would place the emphasis on the word *only*. For truly, God alone, God *only* knows in the infinite sense of the meaning of this phrase. Part of His character, part of His personality is that He is Omniscient or all-knowing. He is never caught off guard, He is never caught by surprise, He never has an "aha!" moment. As one person once said to me, "Did it ever occur to you that nothing ever occurs to God?" He knows past, present, and future. "I am the Alpha and the Omega, the first and the last, the beginning and the end" *(Rev. 22:13)*. "Thine eyes have seen my unformed substance; And in Thy book they were all written, The days that were ordained for me, When *as yet there was not one of them...* Thou dost know when I sit down and when I rise up; Thou dost understand my thought from afar. Thou dost scrutinize my path and my lying down, And are intimately acquainted with all my ways. Even before there is a word on my tongue, Behold, O Lord, Thou dost know it all" (Ps. 139:16, 2–4).

So we can begin to know God by acknowledging that He is there, and that one of the first attributes reserved for Him and Him alone is that of being omniscient or all knowing. Nothing gets by Him, though we would like to think at times that it does. It is not like I can throw a curveball and He is going to miss it. No, in baseball terms, it is a homerun every time, for omniscience means He is always way out ahead of you and me and knows things such as how many hairs are on our heads (though for those who are bald, this is somewhat easier to ascertain!). The psalmist makes it clear that He knows all about you and me, even to when we rise up or sit down, and knows our thoughts before we have them. I would enjoy having

TERRY AYCOCK

this type of knowledge in my relationship with my wife and children, but "such knowledge is too high, I cannot attain to it." Only God has this kind of knowledge.

A LOVING GOD

What makes this knowledge even more profound is that, even with all of this knowledge about His creatures, He is the God who loves us unconditionally. He is God, and He is love. We are told throughout the Bible of His great love and kindness, none more recognizable than that found in John 3:16: "For God so *loved* the world, that He gave His only begotten son, that whoever believes in Him should not perish, but have everlasting life."

Contrast this with what we experience on the human level. None of us knows another human being completely, yet with the knowledge that we do possess, we can be either loving or mean spirited with that information. And our love, most of the time, is not perfectly unconditional. We all have unspoken or hidden agendas, even if they are very small ones. And if moved by events or circumstances, we can take the information we do have and be vicious in our treatment of other people. As the priest told Rudy in the movie by the same name, "In all of my years of theology, I have learned two things about God. One, He exists and two, I am not Him."

In his masterful book on the character of God entitled *Knowing God*, J. I. Packer says this about a loving God:

> God's love is an exercise of His goodness towards individual sinners whereby, having identified Himself with their welfare, He has given His Son to be their Savior, and now brings them to know and enjoy Him in a covenant relation. (Packer, *Knowing God*, pg. 111)

120

He goes on to say that "such an identification is involved in all love; it is, indeed, the test of whether love is genuine or not." He, also, speaks of God's love as being a "holy love." "God's love is stern, for it expresses holiness in the lover and seeks holiness for the beloved." (pg. 110)

God as love is what defines His care for His creation and His creatures, and from that love flows His grace and mercy. It is what sets a relationship with God apart from other religions which claim to have gods or goddesses, or who claim to have a god who is both distant and vengeful, but who does not initiate or show love for those who would worship him or her.

A Holy God

The danger we can sometimes encounter is in emphasizing God's love to the neglect of the fact that, above all, He is holy. Books have been written and analysis given on just what it means to say that "God is holy." We are told several times in the Bible to be "holy as God is holy." But what does that mean exactly?

Have you ever tried to be holy? I mean taken pains to try and be holy, or at least look holy? In attempting to do so, it always comes across—at least on the human side of the ledger—as being self-righteous. Once, when I was in high school and we had just finished a hard basketball practice session, we were walking out to our cars to head on home. We had sweat quite a bit this particular day, run more line drills than humanly necessary (or so we thought), and even after a cool shower, were still sweating profusely through our pores. One of the guys commented that he was "hot as hell." This was my cue. In my most self-righteous tone (I was a churchgoer, mind you), I said, "Well, I am glad you believe in hell, 'cause it sure exists." He turned on me with immortal words I have never forgotten. "Aycock," he said, "half the time you're a little saint and half the time you cuss like a sailor." I am rarely speechless, but this caught me up quite short on words. I had no response and went away, knowing that my attempt at being "holy" only came across as "holier than thou." And he was right. I would be good for about three months and then for three months, it was like the verbal dam burst, and I would join in the verbal exercises we know as "cussing."

Holy, at its root meaning, conveys the idea of being "separate." But God's holiness is more than being separate. As R. C. Sproul points out, God's holiness is also *transcendent.* This means to "climb above, to go above and beyond certain limits." As Sproul says, "When the Bible calls God holy, it means that God is transcendentally separate."

While I could list a lengthy addendum of the characteristics of God (and there are many), God's love and God's holiness are the two that are, at some level, a summation of who God is. Again, we are finite looking at He who is infinite, and even though we could create a box of characteristics, which would be true about who God is, it is God as love and God as holy that drives everything else.

God as love demands that He is a God of grace and mercy and kindness and patience. God as holy demands that He is a God of justice and righteousness and wrath and judgment. Like the old song "Love and Marriage" ("like a horse and carriage, you can't have one without the other"; though our modern post-Christian culture would say otherwise), these two characteristics stand juxtaposed and yet in perfect harmony with one another.

What happens so often in our personal lives and in the life of the church is that we have a tendency to get out of balance regarding how we both practice and teach these truths about God's holiness and love. One of my seminary professors once told our class that life is like a pendulum, and that we would recognize dead center as we pass it by! Our tendency is to swing from one extreme to the other.

Emphasize God as love without the counter balance of His holiness, and we end up with a mush God who will not make demands and who just loves all people so much that pretty much anything goes. We, at this point, like this because sin does not enter the picture, and we can stomp all over God's grace because He just loves us so much.

However, emphasize God as holy without the counterbalance of His love, and we face a God of continual thunder and judgment who is ready to strike at any moment. His demands and commands are not given as an act of love for us, but as a list of rules that we must follow or face the immediate consequences. God is looming around each corner of our lives, ready to pounce. So emphasizing this characteristic without the counterbalance of His love leads us to a harsh, judgmental God for whom we have the wrong kind of fear.

Now here is the real deal. Without a continual reliance on the Holy Spirit, it is impossible to live this kind of balance in our lives. We tend to live the pendulum life, going back and forth from one extreme to the other, judging others at times, at other times, letting it slide in our own lives as well as others. So it is very important to have a moment-by-moment dependence on the Holy Spirit. And let's face it, none of us do this perfectly because of the continual battle we have with the world, the flesh, and the devil.

But this is about God's character, not ours. Sproul once wrote that which I found to be both accurate and profound. Let me quote him at length: "It's dangerous to assume that because a person is drawn to holiness in his study that he is thereby a holy man. There is irony here. I am sure that the reason I have a deep hunger to learn of the holiness of God is precisely because I am not holy. I am a profane man—a man who spends more time out of the temple than in it" (R. C. Sproul, *The Holiness of God*, pg. 33).

All I can say at this point is, "Amen and amen." And to acknowledge that God *only* knows and to be thankful for the knowledge that He knows exhaustively, yet loves you and me enough that He sent

His Son to be that which you or I could never be, in order to comply with the demands of His holiness.

THE FATHER HEART OF GOD

While this is not generally considered to be a characteristic of God, I did not want to conclude this chapter without touching on a very important aspect of who it is that we call "God."

Just the term *God* makes him seem so wholly other that it would seem impossible to have any kind of a relationship with Him. Almost as if He is "out there" and somewhat aloof from His creatures and creation. Yet this is the beauty of knowing that Jesus referred to Him as "Abba Father" and immediately made Him personal and accessible to us. The term *Abba* was a term of endearment and closeness.

Too many in our world today do not have the privilege of having a wonderful earthly father to model for them what the concept of "Abba" father actually looks like in the flesh. And as I stated earlier, it makes it difficult for them to have a healthy image of what the term "father" should mean. That being said, it does not change the fact that our Heavenly Father is referred to in both the Old and New Testaments as being long-suffering, full of kindness and patience, loving those whom He has created, and longing for the relationship with us that we so long for with our own earthly father. And the kind of relationship that a true father longs for with his children. Thus, Jesus refers to the first person of the trinity as "Abba Father."

My own father died when I was eighteen years old and had just graduated from high school. When I headed off to college in the fall, little did I know that God would become very close to me, in time, as my Father, and I came to know Him more that way than I might would have otherwise had my own father been alive. I had a great and wonderful earthly father, so it helped in my own concept of a great and wonderful Heavenly Father, but God the Father became a true father to whom I talked with very often as if He was the "Dad" I no longer had. I had no other father with whom I could talk, so I just talked with Him.

There is so much more that could be and has been written about the attributes and the characteristics of God. C.H. Spurgeon, minister of New Park Street Chapel in Southwark in England, said this as he opened his sermon on January 7, 1855: "The highest science, the loftiest speculation, the mightiest philosophy, which can ever engage the attention of a child of God, is the name, the person, the work, the doings, and the existence of the great God whom he calls his Father" (quoted by J. I. Packer, *Knowing God*, pg. 13–14). I believe that if we can grasp what I have written in this chapter, it would change and motivate our lives at a very deep level. To know that God is omniscient and sovereign should give us comfort in knowing that nothing slips by Him. To know that God is love and holy should ease our minds in knowing that He wants our full worship and obedience while nurturing us along with that love. And finally to know that He is personal and can be referred to as "Abba Father" should give us great comfort in knowing He cares about every aspect of our lives. God only knows what I'd be without Him!

CHAPTER 9

I Know There's an Answer

"If God hath been so engaged in teaching, certainly we should not be negligent in learning; but should make growing in knowledge a great part of the business of our lives."

—Jonathan Edwards
(Christian Knowledge)

"I know there's an answer. I know now, but I have to find it by myself."

—Brian Wilson/Tony Asher

"Answers are there to be found, but we must ask the right questions and be prepared for those answers that will surprise us."

—Anonymous

"We must show the world that Christianity is more than a private belief, more than personal salvation. We must show that it is a comprehen-

sive life system that answers all of humanity's
age-old questions: Where did I come from? Why
am I here? Where am I going? Does life have any
meaning and purpose?"

—Charles Colson

When I was a student in college, I was involved with Inter-Varsity Christian Fellowship on our campus. Each week, we had what we termed our "evangelistic book table," where those of us who participated would pass out free booklets and hope to engage fellow students in conversation regarding a relationship to God through Jesus Christ. I remember having several very stimulating conversations, but one I remember quite well.

A young lady whom I will call Sally stopped by the book table, looked straight at me, and said, "Well, I guess you're going to tell me Jesus is the answer, huh?"

I looked directly back at her and responded, "Well, I don't know what your question was going to be."

She smiled slightly and said, "Ah, that was a good response." She was quite bright and over the course of the next couple of years, we had some very interesting conversations. But my response (and let me be clear, I was not always so quick with a good response) had caught her a bit off-guard and interested her enough to continue on in conversation.

Knowing that there is "an answer" and communicating that answer in terms that are clear and speak to our current world and knowing that more questions will follow is part of what makes the life we live so interesting and so challenging. While there are absolutes that are eternal, there are also those areas of gray that dot the landscapes of our existence. Not that all that we see is a "sad, hazy gray" but along with the absolutes stand the areas of gray.

The crux of Christianity and the Christian message is the issue of truth. It is not how we feel about religion and such things. It is not simply that, "You ask me how I know he lives; he lives within my heart." It is not whether it is one answer among many that could be correct, and most of all, it is not simply pragmatic. A conversation I had recently with a person who was telling me that a minister she knew in New England had said to her that he believed Christianity was true because "it worked" points out the issue and the problem of pragmatic religion very clearly. No, as Francis Schaeffer often pointed out, we must ask if Christianity is true to "what is there." And if not, then we should, by all rights, discard such a belief. However, if it is true and it is truth, then we should grasp it as if our very lives depend on it, for they do.

Pluralism and Modern Culture

If one were to get in a time capsule and go back to the mid 1920s up through about the mid-1960s, at least in Western culture, we would find a far different world from what we experience today. There was a clear sense of right and wrong, regardless of which was being practiced. We had a strong Judeo-Christian base, and even those who did not believe at least understood some of the basic tenets of what that world view entailed. The result, if I can be allowed to simplify somewhat, was that there was not the moral and ethical confusion that we experience today. The lines of morality were not so blurred and culture was appalled at things that today we have come to accept as morally neutral. What has been the result has been that anyone who says that they have "the answer" is looked upon as if he or she has three heads. To say, in our modern culture, that "I know there's an answer" is to appear to be arrogant, a know-it-all, and at worst, bigoted.

Pluralism is widely dominant in Western culture and has been both a blessing and a curse. On the one hand, it has allowed for a wide diversity within our culture, which, in the right context, is a blessing. However, such pluralistic diversity has had the unfortunate result of producing the world view that there is no right or wrong and that anything goes. In other words, complete relativism. Whatever works for you or whatever makes you feel good carry the day. It is made to sound as if we are open-minded and will "live and let live," but the real result has been an underlying chaos in which we no longer recognize any real answers and no longer have a moral and ethical underpinning to our culture.

Listen to our national monologue (not dialogue, which is important) on abortion, adultery, fornication, homosexuality, gun control, etc. and try to find any sense of moral indignation as what we would formerly refer to as sin. Just as one instance of this, how many young people do you know who live together before marriage (if they ever do enter into the marriage covenant) have children and think nothing of what they are doing? "Well, it's just a piece of paper." "Well, you need to try the shoe on to make sure it fits." Other such pearls of wisdom avoid the search for finding meaningful and true answers to the questions of life that will certainly raise their heads in due time.

Most of this has come about because we no longer want to offend by saying we have "the answer." This doesn't mean that life is not complicated, and that such complexities come easily, but rather that, without a moral compass to guide our culture, anything goes and we drift about like a ship lost at sea with no rudder to help guide her. How has this shift come about? Where have the foundations to Western culture gone and how do we recover them?

THE 1960S

Let me be clear (if I haven't already) that this is not a book to answer all critical questions of theology, sociology, psychology, philosophy, and cultural analysis. That would take volumes and a much more scholarly mind than I possess. But I do have some insights and some observations, which are pertinent to the subject at hand.

Others have laid out the philosophical and theological background to what led to the moral collapse we have seen. I will touch on some of that, but my "look back" will be a bit more personal.

I lived through the 1960s as a kid growing up in a small town in Texas. I was far removed from the west coast or east coast goings on that dominated the cultural landscape. I was rather a somewhat casual observer, just trying to figure out life as a kid!

If you were black during the 1950s and 1960s, especially in the South, it was both a horrible time and a time of upheaval. I vividly remember going to the movie theater in my small hometown and seeing the "colored only" water fountains and bathrooms, and the balconies that were for "colored only." Our local swimming pool was for whites only, and when it opened up to "coloreds," the pool emptied of whites and eventually shut down for years. So to say that these were "golden years" would depend on your color at that time.

I watched as the hippie movement developed and protests about the war and culture, in general, became the news stories of the day. Culturally, The Beatles were blamed for the moral collapse of the nation's youth and for leading young people into blatant rebellion, whether through hair styles or living arrangements. "The Fab Four" or "The Mop Tops" unfairly became the lightning rod of the swiftly changing moral fabric of western civilization.

It would have probably been nice if it had been that simple, but the truth is that philosophical undercurrents from influences of existentialism, pragmatism, and nihilism were coming to fruition. The chickens, as they say, had come home to roost! "Question everything" became the battle cry of the cultural elite, and question we did.

Communes became a popular way of escaping from society, each trying to find or build their own utopian society. "Free love" sounded great until children started popping up who needed the love and care of a family, and what they got instead was the tag of being an "inconvenience." What does a culture do when children become inconvenient? They abort them. And all under the guise of a woman having the right to her own bodily decisions. What about the rights of the unborn child, who never asked to be created? Of course, one of my questions was always, Where are the men who helped to create this human being? What happened to their responsibility? At the heart of the pro-abortion movement was not all of the smokescreen that was put out about a woman's right to choose and calling the human actually being formed a "fetus" but instead was the fact that moral and ethical standards had changed, and the basis we once had in our Judeo-Christian values had been challenged and torn away because they did not fit into a culture that wanted to live for pleasure and freedom from any responsibility. You cannot live for pleasure and live an irresponsible life if absolute moral and ethical values are staring you in the face.

So our culture, adopting what author and analyst Christopher Lasch so brilliantly labeled as "narcissism" began to live out the moral relativities that we had come to believe. The basis to establish a free society founded on biblical teaching and moral and ethical living, first established when the Pilgrims landed in Plymouth Rock in 1620, slowly began to erode. Like a slow moving lava flow, all in its path was destroyed and cultural relativity has come to rule the day. And as Francis Schaeffer and C. Everett Koop wrote in 1979, "Cultures can be judged in many ways, but eventually every nation in every age must be judged by this test: *How did it treat people? What was unthinkable in the sixties is unthinkable no longer*" (Schaeffer and Koop, *Whatever Happened To The Human Race?*, pg.15, 17).

I have often said to friends and family that the 1960s was *the* decade that set us on the course we now find ourselves moving. Oh, surely, much more led up to the 60's, and those who have studied the decade can point to previous decades and previous philosophical teachings as being the points of influence that brought about the decade. But the common person on the street, who has little concern with philosophy or world view, got to experience the shift in world view during that decade, anyway, without really knowing the intellectual basis for what was happening. And as media such as television, movies, and, eventually, the Internet began to bombard us with relativity in what it presented, under the guise of objective entertainment, we became more and more desensitized to true moral guilt and that old-fashioned thing previous generations called sin.

Let me illustrate. When *All in the Family* was released as a "landmark" television program, my dad and I watched the first show. I will never forget his reaction. After it was over, he looked at me and said, "That is just trash." The program dared to broach subjects long held as sacred and private and moral, and with Dad, they had crossed a line. I have to admit that I thought (at the time) that he was just reacting because the character of Archie Bunker was too close to his own persona! But my dad had a basis of morality and ethics that he felt had been violated with an "in your face" type of challenge. He may not have understood the philosophical and even theological backgrounds to what was happening, but he, intuitively, understood the shift. In hindsight, it was the beginning of television taking a decided turn.

Movies had already made the turn. My dad had gone to see *Gone with the Wind* in 1936 when it was released, and he told me that there were audible gasps in the audience when Clark Gable spoke his famous "Frankly, my dear, I don't give a damn!" line. Oh, if he were here to listen to what is spoken in movies today!

The swivel on which our modern culture of relativity (some call it "post-modern") turns is the decade of the 1960s. From that decade forward, to say that we "have an answer" became a questionable proclamation.

TRUE KNOWLEDGE

Psalm 53 begins by saying, "The fool has said in his heart, "There is no God." Psalm 10 actually expands on this. "For the wicked boasts of his heart's desire, And the greedy man curses and spurns the Lord. The wicked, in the haughtiness of his countenance does not seek Him. All his thoughts are, 'There is no God.'" So many who scoff at any Christian answers actually are scoffing, not because such answers don't exist, but because such answers fly in the face of what has already been assumed, and that is that God does not exist.

The positions that God exists or that God does not exist are both faith positions. Hebrews 11:1 states, "Now faith is the assurance of things hoped for, the conviction of things *not seen*." And verse 6 goes on to say that, "And without faith it is impossible to please Him, for he who comes to God must believe that *He is*, and that He is a rewarder of those who seek Him." I don't know about you, but I have personally never seen God in any shape, form, or fashion. Oh, there are those who probably believe that, having seen them, I have at least come pretty close, but I am fairly certain that I am safe in establishing that I have never seen the Almighty Creator of the universe!

Solomon, considered to be the wisest man who ever lived, writes in Proverbs 1 that "the fear of the Lord is the beginning of knowledge; Fools despise wisdom and instruction." So where do we find the answers that so many are searching for? How can we say with a strong assurance that, "I know there's an answer"?

The apostle Paul writes to us in his letter to the Colossians the following: "See to it that no one takes you captive through philosophy and empty deception, according to the tradition of men, according to the elementary principles of the world, rather than according to Christ." Now before anyone gets carried away with this verse and starts banning and burning books on metaphysics and epistemology, or the writings of Camus, Sartre, Dewey, Pierce, or Russell, let's be clear that Paul was warning about getting taken "captive" by those ideas, not by knowing anything about them. Paul, himself, was well versed in the Greek and Roman philosophies of his time, as seen by the message he delivered on Mars Hill in Acts 17 known as his "Areopagus" address. He, obviously, had read the poets of the time and knew the arguments presented by the Epicurean and Stoic philosophers. Otherwise, he could not have debated with them in the marketplace. The point is that, in order to have an answer, it is helpful to know how to answer in such a way that real communication takes place. Otherwise, we are doing nothing more than speaking into the air.

Jonathan Edwards spoke of different kinds of knowledge that may be learned, including philosophy, astronomy, politics, and jurisprudence. He concludes, however, by saying "but one science, or kind of knowledge and doctrine, is above all the rest; as it treats concerning God the great business of religion. Divinity is not learned, as other sciences, merely by the improvement of man's natural reason, but is taught by God himself in a book full of instruction, which He hath given us for that end" (Jonathan Edwards, "Christian Knowledge," *On Knowing Christ*, pg. 12). Edwards goes on to clarify this and speaks of two kinds of knowledge of divine truth, *natural* and *spiritual*. "The former remains only in the head... The latter rests not entirely in the head, or in the speculative ideas of things; but the heart is concerned in it: it principally consists in the sense of the heart" (Edwards, pg. 13).

True knowledge encompasses both the human mind and its reasoning powers and that knowledge which is of the heart. Even for the simplest person, the basic knowledge of spiritual matters is not hidden. God has, in His infinite wisdom, made the gospel and spiritual matters simple enough for the most simple of His creatures to understand and complex enough that the most brilliant mind will never have the well run dry. As Edwards said, "The subject is inexhaustible" (Edwards, pg. 22).

Why do I say this? Because knowledge of the kind that tells us that "there's an answer" is not and cannot be limited to only those whose genius unlocks the secrets of the atom and beyond, or can it be so limited that such minds would eventually get bored. And it must be simple enough that one can say with certainty (as did Karl Barth, when asked what he had learned in all of his study of theology), "Jesus loves me, this I know. For the Bible tells me so."

One of the areas of study in the world of philosophy centers around what is called "epistemology." It is the broad study of "how do we know what we know." In very simple terms, epistemology points to the area of knowledge and how we know what we know. That's about as simple as it can be stated. This area of study, however, can be very complex.

A class I had in college on a general introduction to philosophy was studying one area of knowledge and discussing various schools of thought on "universals and particulars." Understand that philosophy fascinated me, but I had a difficult time grasping some of the concepts, in part because each philosopher seemed to have a different definition of what is a universal, what is a particular, and what particulars then made up what universals! One day in class, we were discussing Hume's view, and the professor was saying that Hume saw universals in such a way that the concept of "pain" was only a concept and did not really exist in the world of universals or particulars. This struck me as really stupid, so I raised my hand and asked the following: "So you are telling us that Hume believed that, if I put my hand down on this desk, took a hammer, and smashed my hand, that what I am feeling at that particular moment is not really pain but a figment in my mind because in the world of universals, such pain doesn't really exist?"

"That," said the professor, "is exactly what Hume would say."

"Then," I replied, "Hume was an idiot."

The class and the professor all laughed a good laugh at this. Hume was far from being an "idiot," but he was out of touch with reality in this realm of knowledge. My point was that in the world of knowing, pain is a reality. How do I know? Because the neurons firing off in my brain at the point of impact tell me that such pain is real! I know that I know! Such knowledge, though debated by philosophers, needs no such analysis.

Edwards, a brilliant philosopher in his own right, wrote much and deeply about knowledge, but particularly about divine knowledge. How do we know? How do we have true knowledge? How do we know "there's an answer"? Here is what Edwards had to say:

> Such is the nature of man, that no object can come at the heart but through the door of the understanding: and there can be no spiritual knowledge of that of which there is not first a rational knowledge... If men have no knowledge of these things, the faculty of reason in them will be wholly in vain. The faculty of reason and understanding was given for *actual* understanding and knowledge. And if he have actual knowledge, yet if he be destitute of the knowledge of those things which are the last end of his being, and for the sake of the knowledge of which he had more understanding given him than the

beasts; then still his faculty of reason is in vain;
he might as well have been a beast as a man.
(Edwards, pg. 15)

"God," says Edwards, "hath given us the Bible, which is a book of instructions." In this day and age, full of its scientific reasoning, discoveries, and pride (and, yes, science in proper perspective has certainly provided broader knowledge of our world); in a world living on a slippery slope provided by those who would adopt a Darwinian world view that would say that man is basically good; in a world that has, for the most part, adopted a view that says that absolutes and moral laws and ethical laws are outdated, in just such a world, we are informed, "Behold, O Lord, Thou dost know it all... Such knowledge is too wonderful for me; It is too high, I cannot attain to it" (Ps. 139:4, 6).

I KNOW THERE'S AN ANSWER

In one of the jobs I held in my diverse portfolio of employment, one of the managers I had would sometimes get into nice discussions about religion. His father had been a Southern Baptist preacher, and he had grown up a "PK" (preacher's kid). This manager, however, had rejected Christianity and on several occasions, he would say that he did not believe in God because no one could prove that He exists. We would discuss some of the reasoning and ramifications of holding to that view, until finally one day, I looked at him and asked, "Well, you keep saying there is no proof that God exists. What proof would you accept?" He stopped for a moment, then looked at me and said, "Well, you know, I don't know. No one has ever asked me that and I never really thought about it."

I would love to tell you that he converted on the spot, and that his life changed, fireworks went off, and angels sang the "Hallelujah!"

chorus. This I would love to tell you. Truth is, I have no idea what happened from that point forward. I only know he now had to consider on a more serious level what he said he believed. And the real truth is that such a change would have forced him to deal with a lifestyle change, and I am not sure he was ready to give that up.

Quoting Abraham Kuyper, a nineteenth-century theologian who served as prime minister of Holland, Charles Colson says that Kuyper "said that the dominating principle of Christian truth is not soteriological (i.e. justification by faith) but rather cosmological (i.e. the sovereignty of the triune God over the whole cosmos, in all its spheres and kingdoms, visible and invisible). The *entire cosmos can be understood only in relation to God*" (Colson, Charles; *How Now Shall We Live*, pg. xii, emphasis mine). In other words, to understand how it is that we can have answers to the basic questions of life, the answers can only be understood in light of all of creation's relation to a sovereign God. Whether in business, education, art, music, science, math, philosophy, medicine, or any area of life and living, the cosmological umbrella is essential to having a complete understanding to the questions we have and the answers we seek.

Our modern culture seeks answers in many different and diverse venues. Colson writes, "We all base our lives on some vision of ultimate reality that gives meaning to our individual existence. If we reject God, we will put something in his place; we will absolutize some part of creation" (*How Now Shall We Live?*, pg. 243) For some, the answer comes in the form of drugs. With states continuing to legalize marijuana and looking to legalize other more powerful drugs, the god that some worship will become more and more accessible. For some, they seek answers in one sexual relationship after another, hoping to find an answer to love they so desperately need and seek in all of the wrong places. "Biology," says Colson, "takes the place of God as the ultimate reality, and sex becomes the path to the divine" (ibid, pg. 243). In turning away from God, we will seek to find meaning in those things that ultimately do not satisfy, but which feel good or look good at the time.

Others may feel like they have found their answers in reaching the top in business or sports, but find that once they reach the mountaintop, it is not enough. Temporary answers always leave us in the shallow end of the pool, wading about aimlessly, but thinking we have landed in the deep end of an endless cosmological pool. Ultimately, finite worshipping finite provides no long lasting or permanent answers, and we, either, eventually acknowledge such and seek out Him who created us, or we end up drowning in a shallow pool of nihilism or atheism.

I began this chapter by writing about my experience of working on the IVCF book table. The experience I had with the young lady I met there has more to the story. We continued to meet and correspond over the next few years. We had lively discussions, and I answered her questions honestly and as thoroughly as possible. Sometimes, an honest answer was, "I don't know, but I'll think about it and get back to you." Finally, one day, I visited her at her apartment. (I had let my wife know about it, where I would be, and went with her blessing!) As we talked some more, I finally looked at her and said, "I have been talking with you for several years, and I have always been honest in my answers and forthright, wouldn't you agree?" She agreed that I had been very honest and had appreciated our discussions. I had enjoyed them as well, and she always kept me on my toes. But I looked at her and said, "Your problem is not intellectual. You use that to sidestep the real issue, and that is that your problem is a moral one. You know that in giving your life to Jesus, you will have to quit taking guys in there (and I pointed to her bedroom) and just having meaningless sex." She was stunned. "How did you know?" she asked. "I just know because I have answered all of your questions honestly, and we just never seem to get to the end of them. I like you enough to challenge what is the real reason. What will you do?" She said she didn't know but that it would certainly give her pause.

I add this to say that there are people who have true and genuine intellectual questions, but it seems that so many times, it comes down to a moral issue, and we just would rather have our fun until it is too late. We may know the answers, but just not want to deal with them because they would interfere with our lives in ways that we either are not ready for or that we simply do not want.

WORLD VIEW: FINDING THE ANSWERS

Colson has said it correctly when he states, "No worldview is merely a theoretical philosophy. It is intensely practical, affecting the way we live our lives, day in and day out, as well as the way we influence the world around us" (Colson, pg. 477). What, you may ask, do I mean by "worldview"? James Sire, in his book *The Universe Next Door*, writes, "Everyone has a worldview." He goes on to define what he means by that term. "A worldview is a set of presuppositions (assumptions which may be true, partially true or entirely false) which we hold (consciously or subconsciously, consistently or inconsistently) about the basic makeup of our world" (James Sire, *The Universe Next Door*, third edition, pg. 16).

Expanding on this, Colson writes, "The Christian worldview is more consistent, more rational, and more workable than any other belief system. It beats out all other contenders in giving credible answers to the great questions that any worldview must answer: Where did we come from? (creation); What is the human dilemma (fall); and What can we do to solve the dilemma? (redemption). And the way we *see* the world guides the way we work to *change* the world (restoration)" (Colson, pg. 477).

In a western culture that seems to be increasingly antagonistic toward belief in God and that seeks to discredit the Bible as old writings from ancient men who didn't really understand the world in which we live today, it would be beneficial to remember something that Kierkegaard wrote in his essay, "Either/Or." He wrote, "Each person must choose between God and the world, God and mammon. This is the eternal, unchangeable condition of choice that can never be evaded – no, never in all eternity" (Soren Kierkegaard, *Provocations*, pg. 10).

The Bible says this in Ephesians 2:13–16: "But now in Christ Jesus you who formerly were far off have been brought near by the blood of Christ. For He Himself is our peace, who made both groups into one, and broke down the barrier of the dividing wall... that in Himself He might make the two into one new man, thus establishing peace, and might reconcile them both in one body to God through the cross, by it having put to death the enmity." It is in the person of Jesus Christ that we are reconciled to God, that our world view is shaped by redeemed thinking, and that the answers we seek to the deeper questions of life find their end. As Kierkegaard said, we must choose and in choosing, we can then say with certainty that "I know there's an answer!"

CHAPTER 10

Here Today

"All the virtue that is saving, and that distinguishes true Christians from others, is summed up in Christian love."

—Jonathan Edwards

"All men are our neighbors, and we are to love them as ourselves. We are to do this on the basis of creation, even if they are not redeemed, for all men have value because they are made in the image of God."

—Francis Schaeffer

"Love to God will dispose us to walk humbly with him, for he that loves God will be disposed to acknowledge the vast difference between God and himself."

—Jonathan Edwards

"What's love got to do with it?"

—Tina Turner

"Love is here, today and it's gone. Tomorrow, it's here and gone so fast."

—Brian Wilson/Tony Asher

Writing a chapter about "love" is closely akin to writing about God's holiness. Neither one do I fully understand. Neither one lends itself to any expertise on my part. Knowing about love is one thing. To live in a loving way is a constant, lifelong process. Sometimes, we get it right, and sometimes, we completely blow it out of the water.

The word *love* has many different uses in the English language. In tennis, if you are losing a game 40-love, you are basically taking a good ol' fashioned beating because love means you have yet to win a point. You are nothing. You are zero. Love equals nothing in the game of tennis.

It takes on a different meaning when we are referring to food. "I love peppermint ice cream," we might say. Or, "I love a good steak" or "pepperoni pizza." Just name a food (except for boiled cabbage) and love can be attached to it. The terms "love" and "boiled cabbage" do not deserve to be in the same sentence, much less connected as terms of endearment!

Automobile enthusiasts use love as a term of affection for their cars. What is under the hood, the exterior design, or any number of other reasons will bring a person pure delight. Such a person easily attaches "love" to the admiration of the automobile.

We may use the term love when describing an activity. "I love to snow ski," "I love to paint," "I love watching A&M or Dallas Cowboy football (or pick a team)," "I love to play golf or swim or play tennis." Yes, the word *love* has a wide variety of uses in the English language.

Fortunately, for us, the Bible was not written in English. Contrary to what many movies made depicting Bible stories and Bible characters would lead us to believe (blue-eyed Jesus and all characters with English or British accents!), most of our translations have as their sources Aramaic, Hebrew, or Greek. And Greek, where some of our focus will be, is a very precise language.

LOVE IN MODERN CULTURE

All of us are searching for and are on a quest for the deep felt need we have to love and be loved. Much as how Augustine described the "God-shaped vacuum" that we are all born with that is only fulfilled in a relationship to God, the need for this eternal quest for love looms large in our souls. Whether consciously or subconsciously, this search dominates our need to fill the void.

Unfortunately, Western culture is so inundated with humanistic thinking that our search gets misdirected into areas that ultimately are not fulfilling and that are ultimately harmful to us. As the song says, we are "searching for love in all the wrong places." And our culture is happy to point us to those places.

Much of our music speaks of love, but not a kind of love that is eternal and lasting. Some of the music I have heard blasting from the speakers of cars contain lyrics that say things about women that are shocking in how blatantly abusive those lyrics are depicting the females and what the men want to do to them. I have wondered how the young men listening to these lyrics end up treating the females they date. In a different era, the sexual intent and content was certainly there, but not so blatant. The Beatles encouraged a woman to "drive my car," and the Steve Miller Band suggested that they "like your peaches, want to shake your tree." The Beach Boys suggested the girl and the guy could have "fun, fun, fun, now that Daddy took the T-bird away." Three Dog Night would show the girl "to his garden." The Doors wanted a girl to "light my fire." Shall I go on? Love was rarely equated with anything lasting, but rather equated with feeling good, one night stands, and sexual encounters. Again, searching for love but searching in all the wrong places and with too much short-sightedness for the long-term effects.

Television has shifted so dramatically in my lifetime that what this tells us is how the power of ideas and philosophical shifts in thinking can take place in relatively short periods of time. When Lucy and Ricky in *I Love Lucy* and Rob and Laura in *The Dick Van Dyke Show* were dominating the television airwaves, the *married* couples slept in separate, twin beds. One had to wonder how they ever had children on these shows, but they did. Prime time television today is filled with storylines involving relationships that are nothing but sexual in nature and have very little to do with true love and lasting relationships. Even ones I have liked, such as *Frasier* and *Seinfeld*, relied on casual encounters for parts of their storylines, and real love seemed as elusive as the "elusive butterfly of love," which was chased and sung about in the 1960s.

The cinematic reach of today's movies provides with some excellent movies from time to time, depicting great stories which tug at our hearts and challenge our minds on occasion. Most of the time, however, we are left with movies such as *The Hangover* Parts I and II, *The Ugly Truth*, and *Horrible Bosses*, and a plethora of borderline pornographic fare (for example, *Fifty Shades of Grey*), which treat love as nothing but feelings and sexual situations and leave us walking away feeling violated and empty. Rare are movies such as *The Railway Man*, which deals with cruelty and ultimate forgiveness, or *Unbroken*, which deals with how one can endure such cruelty and severe punishment and not only survive, but live to forgive the captors in a way which shows us the deeper meaning of love and what love entails.

A BIBLICAL VIEW OF LOVE

As I have been writing this chapter, I have realized just how much that culture has shaped my own notions of love. I have listened to as much music as anyone and have watched countless television shows and movies and find that I think about romantic notions of love I see depicted and hear sung about in these songs. In my flesh, I want to experience such romanticism! I wanted to chase the girls on the beach, I wanted to have my California girls, I wanted Rhonda to help me, I wanted my own surfer girl, I wanted my pom-pom play girl! The only such notion that I rejected outright when I heard it came out of the movie *Love Story* and was used for years as a line that resonated with many but was actually quite inaccurate and silly. "Love means," we were told, "you never have to say you're sorry." Even at the time I heard this line (and I was young at the time), I thought how ridiculous it was that anyone would say this and actually believe such nonsense. "I can abuse you, physically assault you, talk meanly to you, threaten you, verbally abuse you, but I never have to say I am sorry because love means I don't have to do so." Ridiculous. Absolutely ridiculous.

Much of what we are influenced by in our culture has to do with love as a feeling. We even have sayings that point us this way: "If it feels good, do it." I don't know about you, but if I based love on "feeling good" or how I felt each day, not much love would be forthcoming. I don't wake up every morning and "feel" like loving anyone, myself included. Based on how I feel some mornings, it is probably a good thing I am not prone to act on those feelings, or I would be in serious trouble.

That is not to say that feelings for someone is necessarily bad or evil. Certainly, we want to feel something for the person and people we love. As much as I abhor how many commercialized days and holidays we celebrate, it is probably a good thing to send a card or flowers or fruit on Valentine's Day to our spouse. We want them to feel loved and special, especially on a day that our culture deems that we better join in on the party or we are in deep trouble.

However, the biblical view of love is much different and much deeper than this, and much more difficult to put into practice. Why is this the case? Simply because the love that the Bible usually speaks of is "unconditional love." There are no strings attached, there is no hidden agenda, there is nothing attached to this kind of love.

When I was a child growing up in my wonderful family, we oftentimes celebrated Christmas with my Dad's brother and sister and their families, and I have some great memories of doing so. We usually drove around to see the Christmas lights on Christmas Eve and attended a Christmas Eve service at the local church. Even as I write this, I can visualize some of those times together with my family, my aunts, uncle, and cousins and truly cherish those memories. The only negative that would make its presence known was that sometimes (not always), the gifts you received would come with strings attached, or so it seemed. I remember receiving one such gift, with the directives of how I was supposed to and had better use it, etc. and thinking I would rather just not have the gift than to have stipulations put on its usage. I never did enjoy that gift thereafter. It affected me so much that, to this day, I work very hard to not attach strings to any gift I give to someone. It is a gift, and as such, should be given "unconditionally."

This is the gift that God gave to us in His Son, Jesus Christ. It is unconditional love. He did not require that you or I be perfect to receive this gift. He required only that I come "just as I am." He did not require that you or I be of a certain economic or social class, or that we could only be gifted and talented to receive such a gift. Each of us, no matter our standing in the community or our positions or our economic situation or our looks or our abilities, has been given a free gift by virtue of God's grace and mercy. We are "saved by grace, and that not of ourselves, lest any man should boast" (Eph. 2:8) This is unconditional love at its very best, at its very finest.

LOVE DEFINED

By no definition of the word *student* was I a great student when it came to languages. Some people, such as my youngest daughter Lauren, are born with a linguistic knack and seem to more easily pick up a different language. She learned Spanish rather easily and can communicate in that language quite readily. We were in Walmart one day, and she started laughing, and I asked her what was so funny. There were two Hispanic speaking ladies in the aisle in front of us, and Lauren told me she was laughing because the ladies had just said something, and she understood everything they just said. When I asked her to translate, she said, "Well, Dad, you really don't want to know." So we left it at that. I, on the other hand, was grateful to just pass Latin in college (and I mean this literally) and somehow managed to get through a year of Hebrew with a B. Greek, on the other hand, was a language that I came to understand was a great language because it was so specific and yet, I struggled with my linguistic knowledge of the language. It was, literally, Greek to me.

Biblical Greek presented me with a better understanding of just how often we miss what the true meaning of a word or phrase is when having it translated into English. It is no wonder we have so many translations of the Bible into the English language, for every translation puts a new or different twist on some of the words used. For example, there are two Greek words for the word *know*, and while our English translation provides us with only the word *know*, the two words have somewhat different meanings. It is helpful to actually understand this when coming upon the word, for it adds more depth and more meaning when this information is known.

By the same token, the word that is translated into our word *love* has at least three different words found in the Greek language. One is the word *agape*, which is defined as love that is unconditional. Another is the word *phileo*, which is brotherly love and from where we derive our word *Philadelphia* or the "city of brotherly love." The third is the word *eros*, from which we derive our word *erotic*, and is defined as sexual or physical love.

In John 21:15–17, we find Jesus asking Peter three times what appears to be the same question. Peter, he says, do you love me? By the time we reach the third repeat of this question, Peter is "grieved" that he has been asked this question three times. What we do not see in the English translation, however, is that the first two times Jesus asks this question, He asks it using a

derivative of the term *agape*, while Peter answers using a derivative of the term *phileo*. The third time Jesus asks, He switches from the agape form to the phileo form, and Peter responds in like manner. Jesus is asking regarding unconditional love initially, and Peter responds with a brotherly love answer. Not exactly what Jesus was asking or looking for. Who knows? Peter may not have been at a point of being able to answer that he loved Jesus unconditionally at that point but did have a brotherly love for Him. But it is important to understand the subtle nuance and how English does not do the passage complete justice because of what is lost in translation.

John 3: 16 uses the word *agapesen* or a derivative of agape when telling us that He so "loved" the world that He gave His only Son. In other words, unconditional love for His creatures. This is what real love is supposed to look like. Unconditional.

Jesus is asked in Matthew 22:36, "Which is the great commandment in the Law?" Jesus answers, "You shall love the Lord your God with all your heart, and with all your soul, and with all your mind. This is the great and foremost commandment. The second is like it. You shall love your neighbor as yourself. On these two commandments depend (hinge) the whole Law and the Prophets." Again, Jesus uses the form of the word *agape*, which fits here for both commandments.

Of course, the well-known love verses come from 1 Corinthians 13:4–7 and uses the term *agape* when describing and defining what it is we call love. We should not be surprised to see how love is described if it is to be unconditional. Love is "patient, kind, is not jealous, does not brag, and is not arrogant. It does not act unbecomingly, does not seek its own, is not provoked, does not take into account a wrong suffered, does not rejoice in unrighteousness, but rejoices with the truth. It bears all thing, believes all things, hopes all things, endures all things." In a word, love like this is an unconditional love.

For many years, I can honestly say that I did not understand or even have a fingertip of a grasp on what this kind of love looked like. What does unconditional love actually look like in reality? I was the recipient of such love from my mom, but that didn't mean I really "got it." Then I had children, then I had a divorce, then I had a daughter who detested me and helped me, without meaning to do so, to understand better what unconditional love looked like for me.

For over twelve years after my divorce, my oldest daughter tested me in ways that I am not even sure she knew about or knows about, but it taught me how to actually practice unconditional love. To say she hated me might be too strong, but she did all she could to sabotage our relationship. Up until that time, I knew I loved my daughter very deeply, but I got a life lesson in learning just a small bit of what our Heavenly Father's unconditional love meant, for I got to practice that very important role as a father who was hated but learned to love without strings, without attachments, without anything coming back in return. Well-meaning friends and family would often give me advice on how I should respond in certain situations, but such responses would not have been loving responses and would have damaged the relationship further. I often said my goal was to have a relationship with my daughters when they were thirty, and that meant responding with love that was truly unconditional. I wasn't always perfect in that respect, but it was not because I wasn't trying. When you are a parent who loves his children very deeply, twelve years is a long time to go without a hug or without an "I love you, Dad." But God was teaching me what His unconditional love for His children was like when He was getting nothing but rebellion and disobedience in return. And when the day came that the hatred was gone and "I love you, Dad" came forth, I can tell you that the wait and the pain and the lessons were worth it, for joy sprang forth like water from a bursted dam. And the joy that she and my youngest daughter bring to my life is way beyond what is deserved or expected, but I'll take it! A relationship restored is worth the effort and worth the wait!

HERE TODAY AND IT'S GONE

In contrast to this constant and consistent type of love, the love described in the song for which this chapter draws its title is one that we are told is "Here today, and it's gone. Tomorrow it's here and gone so fast." This is a love that is fickle and based on the whims of today and the whims of tomorrow, and how we "feel" about the person today and then how we "feel" about them tomorrow. "It starts with just a little glance now. Right away you're thinking 'bout romance now." This may be how we are taught love is supposed to be, but it is a romantic love, a fleeting type of love that is more based on feelings than anything else. And feelings are here one moment and gone with the wind the next.

Several years ago, I had some good friends who, themselves, had gone through a rough marital patch and survived. They told me later (and they have now been married over thirty-five years) that it took them about twenty years before they actually loved one another in the way love is supposed to be. I have had other couple friends who have been married for a long time tell me similar stories and who have said love is not a feeling, but it is something you choose to do on a daily basis, but it took learning some very hard lessons in the midst of the marriage to get to the point of loving in the truest biblical sense. Love, by unanimous acclamation from these couples, is an action verb, not a passive one. It is something you *do*.

Marriage may be the testing ground for how we are to love one another, for there is no other relationship that we have in which the other person knows you and your unique and weird ways so well, warts and all, but it is not the only relationship in which we are commanded to love. In Luke 10:29, a teacher of the law, who had asked Jesus about the greatest commandment and was told, as part of that answer, to "love your neighbor as yourself," further goes on to ask, "Just who is my neighbor?" Jesus then tells the story of the Good Samaritan and asks, "Who proved to be a neighbor?" He points out that the person who acted out of this unconditional love proved to be the neighbor, and he did not even know the man he had helped. In other words, unconditional love is to be practiced toward any and every person.

Do we do this on a consistent basis? Probably not. I know it is so much easier for me to love those who love me back and not those from whom I have nothing to gain. It is easier to love my friends but not so easy to love those who would be considered my enemies. Yet Jesus commands us to love our enemies and pray for those who persecute us. Mother Teresa was a shining example of loving the unlovely with her work among the poor in Calcutta. She was once asked about "success," and she responded by saying, "God does not call us to be successful, only faithful."

The kind of love that Jesus lived out among us and commands us to practice is not an easy kind of love to practice, not an easy kind of love in which to be faithful. This is primarily so because of the sin that so easily besets us. At our cores, even as new creatures in Christ, we battle against the world, the flesh, and the devil, and loving others in the manner to which we are called goes against these three forces. We are selfish, self-centered, and "want what we want when we want it." Our very natures want to lash out at those who hurt us or who hurt one of our loved ones, and we want to exact revenge. Rather than turning the other cheek, our temptation is to fight back, to lash out, to pay back for the wrong done to us. How many times I (we) have made a situation worse by yielding to my sin nature and rather than forgiving and loving the other person. How many times have lived for "pay back?"

Sometimes, there is a righteous anger that arises in us that is justified. Even Jesus threw out the money changers from the temple and overturned their tables because of turning "God's house" from a place of prayer and worship into a place of bartering and economic gain. But this is more the exception than the rule. (I can only remember one time in my own life when such anger was justified, at least in my mind, for it involved a wrong done to my wife and daughter. I never knew I could have the kind of anger that spilled forth, but I realized I was responding to an unnecessary threat to them that needed a firm and certain response.) I know we would all like to use this illustration to justify a lot of what we would term "righteous indignation," but the truth is that such anger is rarely justified. Watch what happens with some men on a golf course, and you can get a good picture of what such unrighteous behavior looks like. Just as such anger kills the enjoyment of playing a good round of golf, so such anger takes a little out of our soul and flies in the face of what it is we are to practice, and that is the love of which Jesus lived and commanded.

A LOVE STORY

I want to end this chapter by quoting extensively and in its entirety a story that Charles Colson wrote about in his book *Loving God*. It illustrates what one man's love for God led him to do and what was the cost for doing so. It is not your typical love story but very appropriate for helping us understand what love looks like.

***

In the fourth century there lived an Asiatic monk who had spent most of his life in a remote community of prayer, raising vegetables for the cloister kitchen. When he was not tending his garden spot, he was fulfilling his vocation of study and prayer.

Then one day this monk named Telemachus felt that the Lord wanted him to go to Rome, the capital of the world – the busiest, wealthiest, biggest city in the world. Telemachus had no idea why he should go there, and he was terrified at the thought. But as he prayed, God's directive became clear.

How bewildered the little monk must have been as he set out on the long journey on foot, over dusty roads westward, everything he owned on his back. Why was he going? He didn't know. What would he find there? He had no idea. But, obediently, he went.

Telemachus arrived in Rome during the holiday festival. You may know that the Roman rulers kept the ghettos quiet in those days by providing free bread and special entertainment called circuses. At the time Telemachus arrived the city also bustling with excitement over the recent Roman victory over the Goths. In the midst of this jubilant commotion, the monk looked for clues as to why God had brought him there, for he had no other guidance, not even a superior in a religious order to contact.

Perhaps, he thought, *it is not sheer coincidence that I have arrived at this festival time. Perhaps God has some special role for me to play.*

So Telemachus let the crowds guide him, and the stream of humanity soon led him into the Coliseum where the gladiator contests were to be staged. He could hear the cries of the animals in their cages beneath the floor of the great arena and the clamor of the contestants preparing to do battle.

The gladiators marched into the arena, saluted the emperor, and shouted, "We who are about to die salute thee." Telemachus shuddered. He had never heard of gladiator games before, but had a premonition of awful violence.

The crowd had come to cheer men who, for no reason other than amusement, would murder each other. Human lives were offered for entertainment. As the monk realized what was going to happen, he realized he could not sit still and watch such savagery. Neither could he leave and forget. He jumped to the top of the perimeter wall and cried, "In the name of Christ, forbear!"

The fighting began, of course. No one paid the slightest heed to the puny voice. So Telemachus pattered down the stone steps and leapt onto the sandy floor of the arena. He made a comic figure – a scrawny man in a monk's habit dashing back and forth between muscular, armed athletes. One gladiator sent him sprawling with a blow from his shield, directing him back to his seat. It was a rough gesture, though almost a kind one. The crowd roared.

But Telemachus refused to stop. He rushed into the way of those trying to fight, shouting again, "In the name of Christ, forbear!" The crowd began to laugh and cheer him on, perhaps thinking him part of the entertainment.

Then his movement blocked the vision of one of the contestants; the gladiator saw a blow coming just in time. Furious now, the crowd began to cry for the interloper's blood.

"Run him through," they screamed.

The gladiator he had blocked raised his sword and with a flash of steel struck Telemachus, slashing down across his chest and into his stomach. The little monk gasped once, "In the name of Christ, forbear."

Then a strange thing occurred. As the two gladiators and the crowd focused on the still form on the suddenly crimson sand the arena grew deathly quiet. In the silence, someone in the top tier got up and walked out. Another followed. All over the arena, spectators began to leave, until the huge stadium was emptied.

There were other forces at work, of course, but that innocent figure lying in the pool of blood crystallized the opposition, and that was the last gladiatorial contest in the Roman Coliseum. Never again did men kill each other for the crowds' entertainment in the Roman arena." (Charles Colson, *Loving God*, pg. 241–243)

So in contrast to what the song tells us (love is here, today and it's gone, tomorrow it's here and gone so fast), the kind of love we are to exhibit, the kind of love this monk exhibited for his fellow men is one that not only lasts but makes a difference in the lives of people and sustains life and relationships in a manner that can only be done when we love God and receive His unconditional love which He has given for each of us. Here and it's gone? No, not ever in God's kingdom.

CHAPTER 11

I Just Wasn't Made for These Times

"Cultures can be judged in many ways, but eventually every nation in every age must be judged by this test: <u>How did it treat people?</u>"

Francis Schaeffer and C. Everett Koop

"The truth of it is that the contemporary culture war evolved out of century-old religious tensions – through the expansion and the realignment of American religious pluralism. It is out of the changing contours and shifting balance of pluralism that the key factors in the contemporary culture war emerge… cultural conflict is ultimately about the struggle for domination."

—James Davison Hunter

"The motives, the processes, the mysteries that made man accept religion and expect God to accomplish what he was unable to do, lead him nowadays into politics and make him expect those things from the state."

—Jacques Ellul

"How can the church give a faithful witness to its Lord and Savior and remain silent in the face of abortion on demand, the breakdown of the family, the idolatry of weapons of mass extermination, and the growing disparity between rich and poor?"

—Donald G. Bloesch

The sentiment expressed in the title of this song is one that I have heard many folks from a previous generation echo, and one that the boomer generation (of which I am a part) is expressing more often. Maybe it comes with age. Maybe it comes with longing for our childhoods. Maybe it comes when we look around us, listen for a while, and marvel at what has happened to a world that once made complete sense. At least it did in our childhoods. The complexities that have surrounded us due to the overwhelming influence of a media that peddles its own agenda and the pluralism and political correctness that dominate our cultural landscape have made the world in which we live confusing and chaotic. Once a nation, once a culture loses its way and replaces a solid foundation based on biblical truth with a foundation of sand based on complete relativistic humanism in which man is the center of all that is, the resulting confusion and an "anything goes" mentality is the certain result.

There is a tendency on my part to become something of a romanticist and think that, *I just wasn't made for these times.* This comes about because I can have this unrealistic fantasy about what it was like in an earlier time, an earlier era, and think that I belonged there. The truth is that I would have been way out of place in the Old

West. I don't even like horses and cows and would have grown tired of walking everywhere and not ever having the absolute necessity of toilet paper. Nor would I have been a fit for the "roaring twenties" and the depression era when people, such as my mom, toiled on the farm, growing their own fruits and vegetables, gathering their own eggs, killing their own chickens and hogs and cows for the meat, and living without indoor plumbing. It is not that I have a toilet or bathroom fetish; I just like some of the modern conveniences like toilet paper and indoor plumbing!

Having said all of this, the fact remains that the Christian consensus has been lost and the times have been and are a-changing. And we find ourselves facing a host of issues that we would have never thought would have been anything with which we would have to deal. So whether or not we believe that we just weren't made for these times, the fact remains that these times are upon us, and the test is going to be whether or not the church rises to the challenge and that Christians hold firm to biblical truth in light of the deteriorating culture surrounding us.

PANDORA'S BOX

The story of Pandora's Box is appropriate for these times. In essence, Pandora opened her box or jar and let out death and all sorts of evil and closed it, leaving only "hope" in the bottom of the box. Today, "to open Pandora's Box means to perform an action that may seem small or innocent, but that turns out to have severely detrimental and far-reaching consequences." While the action of the Supreme Court in 1973 with their decision in *Roe v. Wade*, opening the box for legalizing abortion, was far from small or innocent, it has certainly had severely detrimental and far-reaching consequences. The millions of innocents who have been killed since that time would attest to the consequences of that action.

What has happened to us that our culture has become a culture of death rather than one that upholds the dignity of life? When Dr. Schaeffer and Dr. Koop wrote their book and held seminars in support of the book (*Whatever Happened to the Human Race?*), it was 1979, and the cultural slide was really only in its early stages. Like a snowball rolling downhill, it has picked up both volume and speed.

It has not only done damage to the millions of innocents who have been aborted, but it has done damage to those who aborted their babies. When I was near the end of my college years, I was personal friends with four women who shared with me their own tragic stories of having abortions, and the damage done to them was devastating. One of them shared, through a heavy flow of tears, that no Christian man would have anything to do with her because of what she had done, and she shared the nightmares and the psychological damage it had done to her. No matter how much compassion I could muster, she couldn't stop crying. I have never forgotten that scene.

Christians find ourselves in a unique and perplexing situation. On the one hand, we defend the dignity of human life and fight to overturn the decision made in *Roe v. Wade*. On the other hand, we are also commanded to have compassion and forgiveness for those whom we encounter who have chosen to abort their babies (not fetuses). The balancing of these two roles creates a unique tension, and one that has not been handled well at times. I have read and talked to those who have said that we can't use Scripture, but must use medical data and psychological data to convince our culture of the wrongness of abortion. This underscores just how much that the cultural consensus has moved away from a Judeo-Christian base, for if the teachings of the Bible regarding human value and human dignity are to be disregarded, then other than rather cold and callous data, what kind of basis do we have for making any moral and ethical decisions? As Colson states, "Since traditional notions of morality and social order are largely derived from Christianity, these moral conventions likewise crumble when God is dismissed as irrelevant or nonexistent" (Colson, *How Now Shall We Live?*, pg. 119).

Just how far has this gone? Donald Bloesch wrote in 1984 that, "Christian values no longer permeate society but instead are generally regarded as archaic or even injurious to the social order" (Bloesch, *Crumbling Foundations*, pg. 37). The words of Amos 8:11 should be a chilling reminder of what a loss of these values means to both God's people and the culture at large: "*Behold, the days are coming, declares the Lord God, when I will send a famine on the land – not a famine of bread, nor a thirst for water, but of hearing the words of the Lord.*" And the psalmist writes in Psalms 11:3, "If *the foundations are destroyed, what can the righteous do?*"

Psalm 139 is a magnificent psalm, which exalts the value of humans, and the fact that we derive our value from being created in the image of God. Liberal theology and many who speak of our "spirituality" want to distort this and say that we all have the potential for being "a god" inside of us, and the *imago Dei* gets flipped to mean something that is not true or intended. We have value because we are all created in God's image, but that does not make us "gods." Here is what Psalm 139:13–16 has to say: "For you formed my inward parts; you knitted me together in my mother's womb. I praise you, for I am fearfully and wonderfully made. Wonderful are your works; my soul knows it very well. My frame was not hidden from you, when I was being made in the depths of the earth. Your eyes saw my unformed substance; in your book were written, every one of them, the days what were formed for me, when *as yet there were none of them.*" This passage, alone, should give us pause when considering the true ramifications of abortion.

By now, we have heard most of the arguments in favor of abortion. Such catch slogans as "a woman's right to control her own body," "economic considerations," and "the favor we are doing the potential parents and society" are just a few that have been put forth as viable reasons for aborting. The most significant change made in framing the argument was in calling the unborn baby a "fetus," which takes away the human element and dehumanizes the situation to provide a level of tolerance and comfort. Joseph Fletcher, known as a "situation ethicist," had this to say regarding an unborn baby: "A fetus is a *parasite*, tolerable ethically only when welcome to its hostess. If a woman doesn't want a fetus to remain growing in her body, she should be free to rid herself of the unwelcome intruder" (*National Catholic Reporter 9, March 2, 1973*). This was the situation the Supreme Court was faced with in 1973, and justice Harry Blackmun, who wrote the majority opinion, "acknowledged at the time that if a fetus were a person, then its rights would be guaranteed under the Fourteenth Amendment… The Courts ruled that the fetus is a non-person with no rights at all at any stage of pregnancy" (Colson, pg. 220). Pretty convenient, huh? The "unformed substance," which the psalmist refers to becomes a non-person according to justices wanting to rewrite the law to accommodate a culture that has discarded "archaic" beliefs.

There are cases upon cases, and data upon data showing us the results of what that decision has produced. It is kind of like wrapping a pig in pretty bows and nice packaging. Anyway you wrap it, it is still a pig. By that, I mean that we can rewrite our definition of what constitutes being a human being, we can come up with any number of justifications for killing (rape, incest, saving the life of the mother, avoiding down's syndrome babies, right to control my own body, etc.) but the truth is that we just want to have sex without having to deal with any of the consequences that might occur because we just want to do what we want to do. Let's get real about this. If we were really honest, the overwhelming majority of abortions don't happen to save the life of the mother or because of rape, etc. The overwhelming majority of abortions occur because the dualism we have adopted in regards to our minds and bodies have led us to a logical conclusion and, "this view implies that sexual acts between unmarried people or partners of the same sex or even complete strangers have *no moral significance*" (Colson, pg. 120). And if there is no moral significance, then an unwanted pregnancy is dealt with in the same manner in which we throw out our garbage. Just one more thing on our list of to-do's that we must take care of today, then go on about our day.

Ball of Confusion

The Temptations had it right. "Ball of confusion," they sang. "That's what the world is today. Heh, heh." My first memory of hearing of someone in my school who was a boy and was more interested in boys than girls was something I just thought someone was blowing smoke about just to get attention. This happened in elementary school, and other than giving this anything more than a casual acknowledgement and then ignoring it was about as much as I can remember. Surely, I thought, they are making this up.

Long before the term "gay" was commandeered by the homosexual community, my school song spoke of being "gay and free and happy. Nor courage do we lack. For we're the true defenders of the crimson and the black." I don't know if the school has changed the words to the school song, but it is a shame if they did, for it was an appropriate word for the spirit of the school. To be gay once meant to be happy and carefree. Use the word today and the meaning takes on something totally different.

Years later, when the boy previously mentioned and I were working during the summer for the same employer, we had the opportunity to have a good visit one evening, and I asked him point blank if he was a "queer" and preferred men over women. That was the only word I knew at the time (the *gay* word had not yet come into vogue) and didn't know how to ask it any other way. I wasn't trying to be mean or ugly, but that was the word that was used at the time. I told him I had heard rumors since we were in elementary school and just wondered and figured the only way to find out was to ask him directly. I wasn't trying to judge him; I just wanted to know if what I had heard was true. He denied it and spoke of some psychology he had been studying and so on. I don't remember the bulk of the conversation. Only that he had been clear in denying such a claim. Then two years later, I heard he had "married" his male lover. Some twenty years later, he died from AIDS. Unknown to anyone, I happened to be walking in my neighborhood one night when I saw him being lifted out of a van and carried into his mother's house. I was down the street and in the shadows, but close enough to see how frail he was that evening. He died not long after this.

I also had another friend with whom I went to Bible studies in our hometown and who was involved in the same group on his campus that I was involved with on mine (Inter-Varsity Christian Fellowship). When I was in seminary, I was going to a conference in the city where he lived, and I called him and asked him to meet for lunch one day. When we met, I asked him how his relationship with the Lord was going, and he responded that it was not going that well. He admitted he had had a random sexual encounter with a female in a park, contracted a disease, and became bitter. He said he had started out by looking at magazines, then quarter peep shows, and the sexual fantasies grew to the point that he could not get satisfaction, and the encounter with the female turned him away from females and on to the homosexual world. At the age of thirty-nine, he also sadly died of AIDS.

On a personal level, I have known three men with whom I was personally acquainted who died from AIDS. Two of them attended Bible studies with me. A fourth young man, whom I met when I was living in a college town and whom we met through the church where we were all attending, sat at my kitchen table one day and shared his struggles with homosexual tendencies. I asked him how old he was when he first started looking at pornography, and he was shocked. He asked how I knew. I said that I didn't but had a pretty good idea based on others I had known who had the same struggle. He told me that he started when he was about twelve or thirteen. I remember telling him that day that he needed to grapple and deal with this seriously now or he would never really deal with it at all. He later graduated, moved away, and from what I later heard, became a vocal proponent for gay rights in the very large city where he lived. There is more to this story, as he struggled for several years before just becoming "who he was meant to be." But I was not around for that struggle, so I will have to leave it at this point.

I write all of this so that what follows will be understood in the light of this not being simply theoretical, but something that is personal as well. It is one of the hot button issues of the day, and one which has the potential to be a minefield waiting for any misstep that one can take. It is one of the most difficult issues I deal with and think about because it is not my personal struggle, and yet it is for many, and it is a relational issue, which is very difficult to understand. On the surface, it appears to be cut and dried, yet there are those even among Bible believing people who do not agree. And because our culture has swung so far away from the Christian consensus, the tendency is for the church to follow and not lead, or as I have heard said, to lead from behind.

WHAT THE BIBLE HAS TO SAY

The first time we encounter anything about homosexuality in the Bible comes in Genesis 19. We are told that "two angels came to Sodom in the evening as Lot was sitting in the gate of Sodom." We are then told in verses 4–5, "Before they lay down, the men of the city, the men of Sodom, surrounded the house, both young and old, all the people from every quarter; and they called to Lot and said to him, 'Where are the men who came to you tonight? Bring them out to us that we may have intercourse with them.'" Sodom was an extremely evil and wicked place, and as the men of the city tried to force their way into Lot's place, the angels pulled Lot back into the house and struck the men blind so that they could not find the doorway. What follows this exchange is what is powerful. Verses 12–13 tells us the following: "Then the men (angels) said to Lot, 'Whom else have you here? A son-in-law, and your sons, and your daughters, and whomever you have in the city, bring them out of the place; for we are about to destroy this place, because their outcry has become so great before the Lord that the Lord has sent us to destroy it." Pretty strong words.

We see the issue addressed in Leviticus 18:22, which says, "You shall not lie with a male as one lies with a female; it is an abomination." This is followed up in Leviticus 20:13: "If there is a man who lies with a male as those who lie with a woman, both of them have committed a detestable act; they shall surely be put to death. Their blood-guiltiness is upon them." Again, these are fairly strong warnings and words. Deuteronomy 22: 5 states, "A woman shall not wear man's clothing, nor shall a man put on a woman's clothing; for whoever does these things is an abomination to the Lord your God." Of course, the argument against these laws is that there were in the Old Testament, and should, therefore, not be considered as legitimate for today. After all, there were some fairly stringent laws and fairly stringent commandments given for those who committed adultery or divorce or any number of other acts which were considered immoral.

The point of these verses, however, is not to focus on the place we find them in the Bible, but to point out how the Lord viewed such acts, and He clearly saw them as an abomination and detestable. Keep in mind, there were other immoral acts, such as sleeping with a brother's wife or incest or any form of adultery that He also saw as detestable as well. It wasn't just homosexual activity He was picking on. It was any form of sexual deviation from His plan for there to be sex between husband and wife exclusively. All such deviations were considered to be sin and were to be dealt with harshly.

Having stated this, Romans 1:26–28 makes it very clear in New Testament terms. It states, "For this reason, God gave them over to degrading passions; for their women exchanged the natural function for that which is unnatural, and in the same way also the men abandoned the natural function of the woman and burned in their desire toward one another, men with men committing indecent acts and receiving in their own persons the due penalty of their error. And *just as they did not see fit to acknowledge God any longer, God gave them over to a depraved mind to do those things which are not proper."* Paul writes later in his letter to the church in Thessalonica, "For this is the will of God, your sanctification; that is, that you abstain from sexual immorality… For God has not called us for the purpose of impurity, but in sanctification" (1 Thess. 4:3, 7). He, also, writes in 1 Timothy 1:8–10, "But we know that the Law is good, if one uses it lawfully, realizing the fact that law is not made for a righteous man, but for those who are lawless and rebellious, for the ungodly and sinners, for the unholy and profane, for those who kill their fathers or mothers, for murderers and immoral men and homosexuals and kidnappers and liars and perjurers, and whatever else is contrary to sound teaching."

In America, we live in a culture that has done its best to politicize moral and ethical issues and to try to frame arguments for abortion and gay marriage and homosexual activity in terms of political issues rather than what they are, and that is moral issues. That way, when a pastor or a church makes any statement in regard to these issues that is not in line with the current political or cultural thinking, the threat can be made to silence the pastor or the church. And to be fair, the church has done a fair job of pointing out these areas of sin while ignoring heterosexual adultery and fornication within the church, and the issues of race and race relations and racial injustices. Oh, there are pockets of groups who deal with these issues, but for the most part, they are swept under the proverbial table. Unfortunately, it has been the most liberal of churches that tend to deal with these, but they have no message to speak into those issues because they have become just as secularized as the culture. As Bloesch points out, "It is especially disconcerting to see the church ally itself with some current ideology in the hope of gaining relevance or credibility. Ideological alignments accelerate rather than counter the secularization of the church" (Bloesch, *Crumbling Foundations*, pg. 39).

GETTING IT RIGHT

Where then do we find ourselves when considering gays and gay marriage and gay rights, etc.? What should the church's response be to those who find themselves in the throes of homosexuality and to those who have AIDS? Do we take the Pat Robertson approach and seem to say that every hurricane or storm that hits an area is God's judgment on us because of homosexuals in our land? Or that the AIDS virus is God's judgment? Certainly, there are always consequences to our actions, and Romans 1 points out the depravity that God gives people over to once they have turned away from Him. Maybe he (Robertson) is right or maybe not, but to quote the once popular wrist band movement, what would Jesus do?

Even a cursory reading of the New Testament tells us that the harshest words Jesus had for anybody were for the religious leaders of his day. They were the ones who plotted to kill him, who brought him before Pilate, who railed to have him crucified. And why did they do this? Because they were irate that Jesus would dare to question their religiosity and were jealous because of all that Jesus did during his ministry. It took away from what was happening in the synagogue and put the focus on the true God and the people, rather than on who was the most righteous and who wore the best priestly robes.

Were we to focus on the laws of Moses, as did the religious leaders at that time, there would be massive amounts of stonings and killings of those who broke those laws, starting in our culture with homosexuals. Just look at religious cultures, specifically the Islamic culture, which are today that stringent and do stone or castrate homosexuals and adulterers. The Westbrook Baptist Church, infamous for showing up at funerals of gays and others with whom they do not agree, would fall under this heading. The church, as a whole, must be careful not to fall into the same trap and yet not compromise on truth either. A very delicate balance to achieve.

First, the Bible teaches very clearly that homosexuality is wrong and sinful. Marriage is clearly to be between a man and a woman according to scripture. Let's start there. But fornication and adultery are also sinful, so before we begin throwing stones, perhaps we should be careful to remove the logs out of our own eyes. Though not popular, even in the church, to call sin what it is, we must call *all* sin what it is and not pick and choose. Having established the sinfulness of such behavior, what, then should be next?

Second, the same grace that saved me and those who are in Christ should cause us to extend the same grace to those who find themselves dealing with homosexual tendencies. My wife has been friends with Christian men who struggled mightily with their homosexual tendencies to the point of underlining everything the Bible said about such behavior and wanting to just take their own lives because of the inner conflict. I don't know exactly what Jesus would do, but compassion comes to mind, yet without compromising. It is called "grace." As I heard our pastor say recently, the church now and in the future will need to speak the truth, but speak the truth in love. As Christians further become a minority, truth will become more crucial and should not be decided by a vote of the majority.

But in speaking the truth, it must be done with love and through tears, much like the prophet Jeremiah, who is called the "weeping prophet."

Third, the church must show compassion while speaking the truth, especially for those who find themselves dying with AIDS, but not limited to those in this situation. My wife and my daughters have taught me a great deal about loving people without compromising their own beliefs. They have each had or have close friends who struggle with their sexuality but who have been a part of their lives in very profound and meaningful relationships. It will become more and more important to have meaningful dialogue with one another and to have some understanding about the inner struggle that goes on with dealing with our sexuality. I regret when I was younger that I did not always deal with my friends who struggled with this in a loving, yet uncompromising way. As I said, I have had to learn from my wife and daughters, and some friends, in this regard.

Fourth, it needs to be understood that it is not going to be popular to take the position that such orientation is wrong, is not how it is meant to be. Reading articles and literature written by those who have struggled with this and came away with ill feelings toward the church and Christians puts this in some perspective. The Bible and the church are going to be viewed as stringent and archaic because it doesn't fit into the view that such orientation is okay, that such orientation should be accepted as normal. But as Rick Warren stated in an interview with Piers Morgan, we need to fear God more than we fear the opinions and attitudes of people, and His word is clear in its teachings in this regard.

I have to admit that my mind has a difficult time wrapping around the homosexual mindset because I do not have any inkling of that mindset myself, so I have not had to struggle with what goes on in the thinking of one who has and does struggle. Of course, one reads and listens to all sorts of justifications, and the perceived failure of organizations such as Exodus International and others like them, who came into existence to supposedly help those struggling with homosexuality find their ways out, only tends to magnify the deep problems that exist in the minds of those who are bent this way. It would probably help if Christians would not be so quick to judge and if some in the homosexual world would realize that some of the reaction they receive is because they shove it in the face of the culture and those who are opposed, and resentment builds because of this.

In one of the jobs I worked, it was obvious to all of us there that one of the females was lesbian. Just like each of us, however, she was there to work her job and not demand more rights than any of the rest of us received. She came in, day in and day out, did her job, and went home. She was as good a worker as any of the rest of us but was shunned by some and made fun of by others. Occasionally in life, I do something right. When I resigned and was working my last day, I will never forget her coming up to me with tears in her eyes and saying, "I've enjoyed working with you and am going to miss you. You are the only one here who ever treated me decently. I wanted you to know I'll miss you being here." She gave me a big hug and walked away. I was stunned. I knew her situation, but she never asked for favors, never said her "rights" were being violated, never vocalized her situation, though we all knew. But she deserved to be treated decently. Like I said, occasionally, I do something right.

This should be the normative for we who are Christians. It doesn't mean we agree or that we condone the lifestyle. It is the way that Jesus Christ would have treated people. What would Jesus do? He would love them and die for them. That's what He would do. That's what He did.

A MATTER OF RACE

Long after the civil rights battles were waged in the 1960s, we find that the old adage "Three steps forward, two steps back" seems appropriate for the times in which we live. The charges of "racism" and "white privilege" seem to be the focus of so much that we find our culture confronting. How is the church and how are we as Christians to live and to act in just such a time as the one in which we are living? Or do we simply say, "I just wasn't made for these times?"

I read a great deal of literature that addressed the "black/white" issue when I was in college. Books such as *Black Like Me, The Invisible Man, Talley's Corner,* and *The Autobiography of Malcolm X* were some of the books I read to help me to try to better understand from whence all of the racial tensions originated. And, of course, I have read volumes on the Civil War and those things which led up to the Civil War to try to understand the powerful influence that slavery had upon this country. Christians such as William Wilberforce in England spent the bulk of his political life fighting for the abolishment of slavery, and reading of him and his work in this regard helped to better grasp the pure evil that was the slave trade in both England and America. The book *Roots* and the subsequent television series in 1977 by the same name helped to make the understanding of slavery and the slave trade more personal because of what the author, Alex Haley, was accomplishing in tracing his own family roots.

One would either have to have been completely asleep or totally sheltered in the 1950s and 1960s in this country to have not been aware of the injustices that were occurring to the black population during those times. They didn't start then, of course, but I was alive as a child and young boy during those decades, so I was able to see some of this up close and personal. "Colored Only" or "No Coloreds Allowed" were words I saw posted on movie theaters, public bathrooms and drinking fountains, and public swimming pools. Northerners seemed to think that only Southerners were participants in this atrocity, but such was not limited to only the south. Take note of where much of the national unrest unfolds. It is not in the south. Though the "Emancipation Proclamation" had been passed in 1863 and slavery had supposedly been "abolished" at the close of the Civil War, one hundred years later, we were still very segregated and very much split into black and white in this country.

As we find ourselves in the second decade of the twenty-first century, many of the issues have been addressed and some have been laid to rest, but even with the election of our first black President, we find that the divide can still raise its very ugly head. We have to look no further than events over the past few months and years that have sparked charges of "racism" to find that, in some ways, we are still fighting some of the same old battles. Rather than living the words of Martin Luther King Jr., when he said he longed for the day that "a man is judged not by the color of his skin but by the content of his character," the color of our skin is something that some continue to want to make an issue.

I cannot help but wonder what Jesus thinks about all of this, and what is the response He would hope to find from those of us, black and white, who call ourselves His followers? We throw around terms such as "racism," "racial injustice," and "white privilege," but what do those really mean and what does such terminology actually hope to accomplish? The words themselves are highly charge with emotional and political content. I am not being naïve or trying to downplay the issues that such words represent, but I am not even sure that we really understand what they mean. They come across at times as just catch words or nice sounding words for academia and the cultural elite. And frankly, I have seen prejudice and racism on both sides of the aisle, so to speak, and know that in order for Jesus Christ to be followed and honored, we need to become as colorblind as is humanly possible. I am not blind, or are you if you are reading this, and we would be lying and foolish to say that we don't see color, but that should not be the focus. As I heard Andrew Young say once at a conference I was attending, "Once those folks with the white hoods take the hoods off, underneath, they're just folks like you and me." Black or white, we are all "just folks."

MAKING A WAY

We would do well to remember what Ephesians 6:12 says. "We wrestle not against flesh and blood, but against principalities, against powers, against the rulers of the darkness of this world, against spiritual wickedness in high places." Our common enemy is not the black person. Our common enemy is not the white person. Our common enemy is Satan and his horde of demonic beings who come as "angels of light" but whose goal is to set us against one another and create hate and enmity between people. Our real battle is a spiritual one.

Rev. Jesse Peterson, who has addressed many of the racial issues that face us today and is a black minister in California, asks the question, "So how do reach our full potential and restore our families and communities once and for all?" (*Scam*, Rev. Jesse Peterson, pg. 191) He then goes on to lay out a list of ten "commitments" that would go a long way toward racial reconciliation and easing so much of the racial tensions that exists and that the media fully exploits for their own purposes. Those ten are as follows:

1. Restore God's Order – God in Christ, Christ in man, and husbands as head of the home, taking the responsibility as fathers.
2. Commit to Prayer – "shut up, be still, and let God direct your life."
3. Forgive – the key to transforming our communities
4. Commit to Marriage – the family forms the core of our civilization
5. Judge By Character, Not Color – the battle is spiritual, not physical

6. Become Independent of Leaders – hearts, minds and souls to God
7. Repudiate 'Black Culture' – written to the black community, he states that much of the culture is destructive to the black community. I would add that this applies to the white community as well.
8. Embrace Work and Entrepreneurship – hard work and diligence
9. Commit to Education – getting a good education is a human thing
10. Commit to True Racial Reconciliation – Blacks, whites, and other races can get along as long as each race is committed to true racial reconciliation. Truth is the only way we can be set free." (*Scam*, Peterson, pgs.191–201)

Though Rev. Peterson wrote these specifically for the black community, these commitments would serve all communities quite well and would provide stronger communities and far less racial tension than what currently exists. While such tensions are real, the constant roar of our television sets drumming in news 24-7 doesn't help our situation. Newsmakers have to make news and each story has to be more sensational in order to keep us constantly glued to their stations so that the media can interpret events for us and we don't have to think for ourselves. As we have seen through the years, the media is not always truthful in what they report, but we think because it's on television or in the newspaper or in social media, it *has* to be true.

The real truth is found in John 3:16. This scripture verse is not just some quote that some guy with rainbow-colored hair displays at ball games to make us wonder what he is doing. No, it states very clearly that "*For God so loved the world* (black, white, brown, etc.) *that He gave His only begotten Son, that whosoever* (black, white, brown, etc.) *believes in Him should not perish but have eternal life.*" This is the truth, and it is in this understanding of why Jesus came that true reconciliation will take place, and that the racial divide that exists will find a way to look beyond color and see each of us for what we are: human beings with a common and unified need for redemption.

In Conclusion

The issues of abortion, homosexuality, and race will continue to be cultural issues with which we will deal. If for no other reason, politicians and the media will make sure of it. As our culture further slides into one that rejects the Christian message and these issues are politicized so to keep the focus off of the moral dilemma they pose, Christians will need to become wiser and more shrewd and will need to have a much greater knowledge of biblical truth than we now possess. Beyond this, the moral message we will need to speak into our culture will need to be tempered with a great deal of love and mercy and grace, for the opposition to our message will become greater and more intense in the days ahead. You need to spend only a small amount of time on social media to discover just how intense this opposition is already to know that, as the slide continues, it will only progress in its intensity.

There are times when I truly agree with the sentiment of the title of the song and the title of this chapter; I just wasn't made for these times. I liked *Leave It to Beaver, Ozzie and Harriet, Mayberry, The Cosby Show*, baseball, Mom, and apple pie. I liked simpler times. But no matter how much I may have liked all of these things, we are not living in those times, and these times will call for living with conviction accompanied by love and grace. And living in these times is just what we were made for. As the words to the song said, "I keep looking for a place to fit in, where I can speak my mind." Now is the time; here is the place. Be thankful and embrace it, for we are here now for the purposes that God has for each of us.

CHAPTER 12

Pet Sounds

"The final choice for modern man is between Christianity and nihilism, between the Logos of God and the ultimate meaninglessness of life and the world."

—Carl F.H. Henry

"For the word of God is living and active, sharper than any two-edged sword, piercing to the division of soul and spirit, of joints and of marrow, and discerning the thoughts and intentions of the heart."

—Hebrews 4:12

"It turns out that there are some things that don't change. God doesn't change: He seeks and saves. And our response to God as He reveals Himself in Jesus doesn't change: we listen and follow. Or we don't."

—Eugene Peterson

"At the end of the day, when I am lying in bed and I know the chances of any of our theology being exactly right are a million to one, I need to know that God has things figured out, that if my math is wrong we are still going to be okay."
—Donald Miller

Legend has it that while Rome burned and Nero played the "fiddle," Christian theologians were debating how many angels could dance on the head of a pin. When I first heard this story, I thought, *Good grief, that's about right*. As the world burns, Christians are arguing about minutia that doesn't really matter. Whether that legend is true or not, it does serve to point out part of the problem.

It does seem to be the case that, at times, we get all knotted up over things that, ultimately, don't matter. Think not? Sit in someone's seat or pew, park in someone's parking spot, use something other than KJV, NIV, or NASB, change the times of worship and Bible study, change the side where the pulpit has stood for years in the church; do any of these and watch what happens. We just seem to get bent out of shape over the most trivial of things.

What I want to propose in this chapter is to present those areas in Christian doctrine and theology that are non-negotiable and those that are negotiable. In other words, provide some guideline that gives us parameters, which allows us freedom on the one hand, and on the other, identify that which is *not* trivial and where we must take our stand.

As I lay these out, I realize that not everyone will agree on my own "pet sounds" or non-negotiables. And not all will agree on those areas which may be areas of which we are free to disagree and still remain friends and Christian brothers and sisters. That is okay. I do believe, however, that if one calls him or herself a Christian, there are certain beliefs that must be held. As I heard the late Keith Green say one time, just going to church and sitting on a pew doesn't make one a Christian any more than going into McDonald's makes someone a Big Mac!

PET SOUNDS (NON-NEGOTIABLES)

In thinking through what the list of non-negotiables should be, there is something of an order to how this list should read. That is, one should follow the other. So before briefly explaining each of these beliefs, I will lay out this list before you. They are as follows:

1. The Bible As the Sole Authority in Faith and Practice
2. The Fall of Man – Original Sin – Sin Enters the World
3. Virgin Birth – Jesus Enters the World Sinless
4. Salvation – Grace through Faith-Cross of Christ Plus Nothing
5. Deity of Christ – Manhood of Christ
6. Second Coming – Jesus Is Coming Again
7. Primacy of the Ten Commandments

As I said previously, not everyone will agree on this list. I have chosen the ones on the list, however, for it seems that these are at the crux of what it is that a Christian should believe and hold to if calling him or herself "Christian." Some might question, for example, the inclusion of the Ten Commandments on this list, but without the "law," how would we have a clearer understanding of both sin and grace? When God gave Moses these commandments, it was pretty clear that these were not negotiated as something that either the children of Israel or future generations of Abraham's heirs (including Gentiles) could bring back to the table and say, "Well, what about coveting someone's wife or possessions. Can we have some wiggle room here?" Or killing, stealing, committing adultery, worshipping other gods or idols, or honoring the Sabbath. There was no "fudge factor" built in to these commandments. Thus, they are called commandments and not—as Ted Koppel so brilliantly addressed in a speech several years ago—suggestions. So I have included them in the list of non-negotiables.

These seven beliefs serve to summarize what it is that is at the core of Christian theology and doctrine. This is not systematic theology, which goes into much more detail and which uses much different and more academic language to define and systematize doctrine. It is important, however, that believers hold to truth and to sound doctrine and equally as important that we understand that we must hold to such with a great deal of love and grace and mercy and understanding. We can be "dogmatic" without being "dogmatic." That sounds contradictory, but what I mean is that we can hold on to truth without being ugly about it. The world, Schaeffer wrote, has the right to judge Christians on the basis of what it sees in our love for one another. It is, he said, the "mark of the Christian." And sometimes, we are just plain ugly in how we go about holding to our doctrines. So as I move forward, understand that while these beliefs are crucial, they are crucial as to not only *that* we hold them but *how* we hold them. Remember, it was Jesus who, when asked the most important commandment, said it was to love God with all of your heart, mind, and soul, and to love your neighbor as yourself.

NEGOTIABLES

Before moving forward with the previous list, I want to lay forth those areas that are some of the negotiables that Christians are going to find themselves disagreeing. There are, no doubt, more areas that may be mentioned, but these areas are ones that seem to get the most print or attention. They are as follows:

1. Church Government – Elder Rule, Deacons, Congregational Rule?

2. Rapture and Second Coming – Is there a rapture?
3. Israel and the Church – the same or separate?
4. Creation – Six Days: literal or figurative?
5. Women's Role In The Church
6. Which Church (Denomination) is Right?
7. Divorce and Remarriage
8. Baptism – Infant, Conversion?

Once again, there will be those who would disagree with this list. For example, divorce and remarriage is fairly cut and dried, isn't it? Or is it? Nothing is said by either Jesus or Paul or the New Testament writers about physical or emotional abuse in a marriage, so what do we do with this? So there will be disagreements in these areas mentioned, but neither salvation nor fellowship is at stake when we disagree, or at least they shouldn't be. That being said, some would consider it heretical to question whether creation was a literal six day event or not. I have my own belief on this and will touch on it later, but my point is that we may disagree and disagree strongly, but we can do so in an agreeable fashion.

The Non-Negotiables

The Bible as Sole Authority. Turn on just about any television show or talk show or news station and what will stand out is the elevating lack of concern for and respect of authority. Of any kind. Parents in sitcoms and dramas are depicted as bumbling fools who allow their children to disrespect and run over them in any number of ways. Authority is out of fashion and politically incorrect. And then we wonder why there is such disrespect and violence occurring at an alarming rate.

When a culture has turned its back on a basis of authority, when moral relativity and confusion seems to be the rule rather than the exception, then that culture has reached a critical juncture in its history.

What a confusing time this is in which to live in Western culture! We applaud those who change their gender and label every event that occurs with the wide brush strokes of racism and white privilege. We debate on just exactly what marriage is and who can marry who, as if that should even be a question. The recent Supreme Court decision has made it legal for same sex marriages and have, in essence, taken it upon themselves to redefine marriage for our culture. We scoff and laugh at those who would admit to virginity before marriage as if there is something psychologically wrong with them. Drug and alcohol use and abuse seems to run rampant, and addiction to pornography, especially with the easy access we now have due to the Internet, is out of control. As we plunge deeper into this moral and spiritual morass, it is clear that, unless something occurs, chaos is around the corner. When every person will do what is right in their own eyes. Where is our basis for authority and how is this slide down the slippery slope halted?

C. S. Lewis was wise in making a distinction between the church and the culture. He stated that we may have legislature of morality and ethics in the true church but cannot expect to impose them on the world. The world is not the church and does not follow Christ. But in the church, we should expect to operate by and be held accountable to God's standards. By simply doing this within the church, we would stand to shake the world. However, we must have a final authority and that final authority is God's word.

Second Timothy 3:16 tells us that, "All Scripture is inspired by God and profitable for teaching, for reproof, for correction, for training in righteousness." Isaiah 40:8 says, "The grass withers, the flower fades, but the word of our God stands forever." Psalm 119:105 states, "Thy word is lamp to my feet, and a light to my path." John 1:1 plainly states, "In the beginning was the Word, and the Word was with God, and the Word was God." Second Peter 1:20–21 tells us, "No prophecy of Scripture is a matter of one's own interpretation, for no prophecy was ever made by an act of human will, but men moved by the Holy Spirit spoke from God."

There are those who would argue that I am making the case for the Bible as sole authority from the Bible itself, which would seem to negate the argument. How can one say that something is authoritative when quoting from the authority itself? But isn't this exactly what Jesus did when making claims of being the "Son of God" and being on a par with God the Father? In John 5:31–33, 36–37, 39 Jesus says, "If I alone bear witness of Myself, My testimony is not true. There is another who bears witness of Me, and I know that the testimony which He bears of Me is true. You have sent to John, and he has borne witness to the truth….the works which the Father has given Me to accomplish, the very works that I do, bear witness of Me, that the Father has sent Me. And the Father who sent Me, He has borne witness of Me… You search the Scriptures, because you think that in them you have eternal life; and it is these that bear witness of Me." Jesus appealed to His works, the Heavenly Father, and Scripture as proof of His own divinity.

By the same token, the Bible makes claims within its pages that it is the authority by which we are to live. The verses I have quoted earlier indicate just what the Bible says about its own inspiration and authority. Of course, there are those who have wanted to add to this authority. The Book of Mormon is put on this same level by those who follow Joseph Smith, and the Koran is put on an equal, if not higher, level of the Bible by those who follow the prophet Mohammed.

Many books have been written that address the canonicity of the Bible or how we got our Bible and what gives the sixty-six books contained within their authority. I would recommend *A General Introduction to the Bible*, written by Norman Geisler and William E.

Nix. I would also recommend *The Books and the Parchments*, by F. F. Bruce. These two books help in understanding how we got the Bible and what was entailed in establishing the canon of Scripture. Suffice it to say, God used people, empowered by the Holy Spirit, to write to us what He needed us to know in order to know Him and in order to know and understand how our sins are dealt with and how we are forgiven. I am simplifying, of course, for there is so much more that He revealed, but He revealed more than enough for us to know Him and to have the authority we need in order to live in a world that needs His love, His direction, and His moral and ethical guidelines. There will always be those who will not accept this and who will want to argue about the authority of an "ancient book" written by "old men," but that is to be expected. The Bible is what it says it is, God's Word, and it is our sole authority in faith and practice.

The Fall of Man – Original Sin – Sin Enters the World. I wrote more extensively about this in chapter 1. It is important for our purposes here because without a knowledge and understanding of this doctrine, we miss the reason "salvation" is even necessary. If there is no sin, if such a story as what we have in Genesis 3 is a fairy tale and makes only for good reading, then Jesus died on the cross needlessly. And His suffering and shedding of blood was a cruel and totally uncalled for act of barbarism on the part of those who participated in his scourging and death on the cross.

However, Romans 5:12 tells us that "therefore, just as through one man sin entered into the world, and death through sin, and so death spread to all men, because all sinned." Romans 6:23 further clarifies that "for the wages of sin is death, but the free gift of God is eternal life in Christ Jesus our Lord," and Hebrews 9:22 says that "without shedding of blood there is no forgiveness."

I once heard a Methodist pastor of a very large church in a big city here in Texas preach a sermon in which he scoffed at the very idea of the "shedding of blood" and basically called this a myth and "grotesque" due to its very nature, and I wondered why he was preaching and just exactly what Bible he was reading. It may seem grotesque and cruel to us, but because God demands a penalty to be paid for sin, the "shedding of blood" was His price, and because it is clear that sin entered the world, God "gave His only begotten Son" to shed His blood as the satisfaction for the penalty that had to be paid. So the doctrine of the fall and original sin is central to why Jesus Christ came and died for us in the first place. Without this foundation to our understanding, then His death on the cross makes no sense and was needless. It is, I believe, a non-negotiable basis to our faith.

The Virgin Birth – Jesus Enters the World Sinless. Following closely on the heels of the fall is the teaching of Scripture that Jesus was born of a virgin. If one takes an anti-supernatural view, the validity of a virgin birth is called into question. How, one with this view asks, is it possible for a virgin to become pregnant? Biologically, they would say, this is impossible. If we all agreed with this view, we would come to the same conclusion and believe the teaching of the "virgin birth" is a myth. However, Scripture clearly tells us that Jesus was born of a virgin and, thus, was born without sin.

Luke 1:26–38 tells the story of how Mary was informed by the angel, Gabriel, of just what was about to happen and told how this was to happen. Mary even asked, "How will this be since I am a virgin?" Gabriel then proceeds to tell Mary how she will become pregnant with child, the child we know will be named Jesus. In the Old Testament, Isaiah 7:14 foretells this story very clearly. "Behold, the virgin shall conceive and bear a son, and shall call his name Immanuel."

This teaching is important because the sacrificial lamb, so to speak, had to be without blemish. If this is so, then the child could not come by normal means, by normal human relationship in regards to pregnancy. Thus, the only way for a sinless child to come into this world would have to be through a virgin. Otherwise, there is no path to salvation; there is no perfect sacrifice to take the place of a sin-filled world that would satisfy the Heavenly Father. This is why this teaching is so crucial to the rest of the story and why, without it, there is no story to tell.

Salvation – Grace through Faith/ Christ and the Cross Plus Nothing. At the very core of what is essential to the message of the gospel is that salvation comes by grace through faith and the finished work of Christ on the cross plus *nothing.* This salvation is unmerited, it is not earned, it is not gained or sustained by any works that anyone might do, it is not based on any righteousness on our part. It is solely based on the finished work of Christ on the cross, and the grace and mercy by which God chooses to save a person.

The book of *Romans* makes it very clear that the law does not save; it serves to point out our sin and our need for salvation, but Paul makes it clear that salvation comes by God's grace and by the finished work of Christ on the cross. *Ephesians 2:8–10* serves as further clarification. "For by grace you are saved through faith, and that not of yourselves. It is the gift of God… not by works, lest any man should boast." Salvation comes at a cost, but that cost was paid by Jesus Christ and his death on the cross. When Jesus proclaimed, as he hung on the cross, that "It is finished," he was stating what Paul and the writers of the gospels make very clear, and that is that salvation comes through the "finished" work of Christ on the cross plus *nothing.* This is the very core of the Christian faith; that salvation is through Christ alone and comes by the gift of God through His love, grace, and mercy. You nor I can ever earn our way into heaven by any merit of our own, by any works of our own, by any righteousness of our own, by anything of our own.

Jesus further makes it clear in *John 14:6* that there is *no other way to heaven, to the Father* except through Him. "I am the way, the truth, and the life" he says. "*No one* comes to the Father except through me." And that way is the way of the cross and through his death and resurrection.

Deity of Christ – Manhood of Christ. One of the more complex mysteries that is difficult to wrap our minds around is that Christ was both divine and human, all at the same time. How, we wonder, can a man be deity? And on the other hand, how can a deity be human? How can they both be occurring at the same time? This teaching and the teaching of the Trinity are two of the most mysterious and complex teachings of the Bible because we have no point of reference as to how to frame such teaching so that it is completely understood.

For example, when considering how God can be "Three-in-One," the only illustration I have ever come upon that came close to giving me some understanding of how this can occur is the comparison of H2O. H2O has the capacity to be a liquid (water), a solid (ice), and a vapor (gas). It has those chemical properties that allow it to be a three-in-one, so to speak. But we have no other point of reference that can allow such a comparison to explain, at least partially, both the deity and humanity of Christ. That is because it is a once in an eternity event!

The Bible clearly refers to Jesus as the Son of God and the Son of Man. Lewis Sperry Chafer states that, "The Deity of the Son is asserted in the Bible as fully and as clearly in every particular as is the Deity of the Father or the Spirit. On the other hand, the humanity of the Savior is as dogmatically set forth" (Chafer, *Systematic Theology*, Vol. 1, pg. 330). Charles Hodge says, "From the nature of the work which He was to accomplish, it was necessary that He should be at once God and man. He must participate in the nature of those whom He came to redeem; and have power to subdue all evil, and dignity to give value to his obedience and sufferings" (Hodge, *Systematic Theology*, Vol. 1, pg. 483).

The Son of Man is referenced in several passages in the New Testament. Matthew 8:20 shows Jesus referring to himself as the Son of Man. Matthew 9:6 finds Jesus saying, "But in order that you may know that the Son of Man has authority on earth to forgive sins," showing in that one statement both his humanity and his divinity. John 5:27 has Jesus stating his authority to "execute judgment because He is the Son of Man." Philippians 2:9 says that "and being found in appearance as a *man,* He humbled Himself be becoming obedient to the point of death, even death on a cross." Beyond these verses, however, we see throughout the gospels Jesus doing very human things such as walking up the mountain, sailing in a boat, teaching in the synagogues, being a carpenter's son, or bleeding as only a human can, weeping at the tomb of Lazarus, and being hungry after forty days of fasting. These are all very human endeavors and emotions.

However, the Son of God appears as well throughout the New Testament. John 3:16 says, "For God so loved the world that He gave His only begotten Son." Peter responds to the question Jesus asks about who the disciples believe him to be by saying, "You are the Christ, the Son of the living God" (Matt. 16:16). Mark 5:7 shows that even the demons knew, believed, and called Jesus the "Son of the Most High God." In Mark 14:61–62, when asked by the high priest, "Are you the Christ, the Son of the Blessed One?" Jesus answered, "I am; and you shall see the Son of Man sitting at the right hand of power, and coming with the clouds of heaven." Colossians 1:19 says that "it was the Father's good pleasure for all the fullness of *deity* to dwell in Him." Jesus healed many, cast out demons, and as John says at the end of his gospel, "And there are also many other things which Jesus did, which if they were written in detail, I suppose that even the world itself would not contain the books which were written" (John 21:25). John had obviously never been in a large Barnes & Noble, but the point is that Jesus did far more in his divinity during his time on earth than has been recorded that we can have great faith in both his divine nature and his human nature.

One cannot claim to be a follower of Jesus Christ and not recognize both the divinity of Christ and the humanity of Christ. Both are necessary for salvation, for without divinity, there is no perfect sacrifice, and without being human, there is no understanding or identifying with perfect clarity the plight of all humanity. This, too, is crucial to the truth of Christianity and the truth of the cross.

The Second Coming of Christ. An earlier chapter dealt with the different views involved in eschatology and the Second Coming of Christ. Since Jesus made it clear that He is coming back again and that believers are to be ready and waiting and watching for His return, the belief in the Second Coming is rather important to the central teaching of Christianity.

Matthew 24:29–31, 42–44, Mark 13:24–27, Luke 21:25–28 are some of the passages of Scripture that speak of the return of Christ. Acts 1:11 makes it clear that Jesus will return and in the same manner in which the disciples saw Him ascend into heaven. Revelation 22:7, 12–13, 20 are all verses in which Jesus tells us He is coming again and coming "quickly." The Jews at the time of the First Coming of Jesus were looking for a king who would destroy their oppressors (Rome) and would lead them as a political and religious king to conquer all who would challenge them. The view that Scripture gives us is much broader than this, and we know that when Jesus came the first time, it was to be the "sacrificial lamb" and servant-Lord. When He comes again, it will be as Lord and King over all of the new heavens and the new earth, and the fulfillment of the role that the Jewish people were expecting the first time around will be fulfilled to a far greater extent than they ever imagined! He will rule over all and "at the name of Jesus every knee should bow, of those who are in heaven, and on earth, and under the earth, and that every tongue should confess that Jesus Christ is Lord, to the glory of God the Father" (Phil. 2:10–11).

The Primacy of the Ten Commandments. Some may wonder why I would add a belief in the Ten Commandments as crucial to being or calling oneself a Christian. *James 2:10* tells us that "For whoever keeps the whole law and yet stumbles in one point, he has become guilty of all," and *Isaiah 64:6* states that "All of us have become like one who is unclean, and all our righteous deeds are like a filthy garment." In *Romans 3–8*, Paul goes to great lengths to clarify why we are not justified by works of the Law, and yet, also, clearly teaches that the Law is not nullified, but is there to point out our sin. Otherwise, how would we know so clearly?

The commandments that God gave to Moses on Mt. Sinai are not necessary for salvation, but without them, such a need for salvation might become confusing and thought to be unnecessary. From what are we being saved? Without the Law, we have no point of contact that tells us just what God expected of us if we were to be "perfected." And when Jesus was asked what the greatest commandment in the Law was He did not respond by quoting any of the Ten Commandments, but what *Deuteronomy 6:5* summarized as being at the heart of the commandments. If Jesus found it important to get to the heart of the matter by answering the question in the manner in which he did, it would seem that the commandments would still be important enough to adhere to in our own time. Jesus also pointed out that He had not come to "abolish the Law or the Prophets; I did not come to abolish, but to *fulfill*" (Matt. 5:17). Again, not that any of us could ever be made righteous by perfectly obeying the commandments (which we cannot and will not ever do), but these point out both the problem (sin) and the solution (obedience). Even Jesus called for us to obey Him and our Heavenly Father, and certainly, the Ten Commandments would serve to be a part of what such obedience would entail.

Does one obtain salvation by perfectly obeying the commandments? No, because Jesus died on the cross as the perfect substitute for our sins, and only His righteousness could ever satisfy the requirement of atonement. So salvation does not come by the commandments or the Law, but without the Law, we would have no account-ability for nor knowledge of sin. And with that knowledge of sin, we must have a way out in order for salvation to happen, and that comes only by the substitutionary atonement of Jesus Christ on the cross. Thus, the need for the knowledge of the Law (the primacy of the Ten Commandments) should be included as a "non-negotiable" for one who calls him or herself a follower of Christ.

THE NEGOTIABLES

The list of negotiables I have listed will be of some concern to some who are very dogmatic about such things as church gov-ernment, baptism, divorce and remarriage, and women's role in the church. There are those who are absolutely certain that their view is the only truly biblical view, and that all others are misguided at best, and false teaching and heretical at worst.

There are arguments to be made from all sides, and it is why it is so important that we do not get caught up in being dogmatic on those things in which there is sometimes just a disagreement on how we see it because of our own grids through which we view such things and our own personal starting points which come with the territory, so to speak.

The fact is, I do not intend to go into a great deal of discussion or detail on the negotiables. There are volumes written on each of these topics, and it is not my purpose to create yet another volume on each area I have mentioned. To further understand the background as to how we have come to the different views of some of these and other important teachings and doctrines of the church, I would sug-gest three books which are more academic in their content, but which serve to help us understand the backgrounds. They are *Early Christian Doctrines* (J. N. D. Kelly), *Documents of the Christian Church* (Henry Bettenson), and *Contemporary World Theology: A Layman's Guidebook*

(Harvie M. Conn). While the church was in its infancy and early formation, teachings such as the Trinity, baptism, communion (one of the sacraments), church government, etc. weren't simply formulated overnight and agreement reached on all fronts. Quite the contrary! These dogmas and doctrines took centuries to determine, and even then, there was not and has not been complete agreement.

Let's take church government as one example. Baptists believe in congregational rule or a democratic form of church rule in which the congregation votes on the direction of the local church. Presbyterians adhere to elder rule, in which the direction of the church is led by elders appointed by leaders in the church. While there may be input from the congregation, the ultimate decisions are made by the elders who have been appointed. Methodists may be democratic on the local level on some matters, but pastors are appointed by a board in each conference. While there, again, may be some input by a local congregation, the decision to move a pastor is ultimately in the hands of the conference board. Within these and other denominations and independent churches, there are variations within for each form of church government. Catholicism is an entirely different form of government with a large, bureaucratic mechanism in place which appoints priests, bishops, and ultimately, cardinals and popes.

Which is correct? All believe they have the correct form of government, but understand that these views that developed were not developed overnight. There are reasons why each group moved in the directions that they did.

Baptism is another example of the wide divergence of views that exist, and each view quotes Scripture to support its belief. "Infant baptism" is believed by some to have a regenerative effect. My parents had me baptized as a six-week old infant because the church we attended believed in this manner. Others believe that without water baptism that salvation does not and cannot take place. They deem it a necessary condition before salvation can occur and will argue very strongly that this view is the only biblical view that exists. Still others believe that baptism can be "sprinkling," while others believe that baptism is done in obedience to one who has been saved and must be fully immersed, signifying our identification with the death and resurrection of Christ. Salvation, according to this view, is not in the baptismal water, but has already occurred prior to baptism. Such baptism is seen as an act of obedience rather than an act of salvation.

The view of women's role in the church is another area of wide divergence that exists in the modern day church. Some believe that Paul was very clear that women are to keep silent in the church (1 Corinthians 14:34–35, 1 Timothy 2:11–15), while others refer to passages such as Romans 16:1-3, 2 Timothy 1:5, 2 Corinthians 16:19 to point out the leadership that women provided in the early church, and without whom, the church would not have made the advancements that it did. How much of the views that were and are espoused are cultural in nature and how much is biblical is difficult to determine. Nonetheless, within churches and denominations today, there is disagreement over what the role of women should be, and whether or not those roles include being pastors or elders or deacons.

If one would like to start a really intense argument, then begin discussing whether or not such an event as the rapture occurs! There are two basic views that exist regarding this teaching. One is that there will be a rapture of the saints before the Great Tribulation and the second is that there will not be any such event happening. Even among those who hold to a rapture, there is disagreement as to exactly "when" such an event will occur. There is the pre-tribulation view that holds that the rapture occurs before the Great Tribulation. There is the post-tribulation rapture that believes it occurs *after* the Tribulation. And there is the mid-tribulation rapture in which it is believed that the event happens in the middle of the Tribulation. And of course, there is the view that no such event as the rapture ever occurs, but rather all such teaching is heresy and that the passages used to build a case for the rapture are really only referring to the Second Coming. One thing is certain: we will all eventually know which view was correct!

Another area of disagreement which exists is whether or not Genesis 1–11, and especially Genesis 1, is to be taken literally as to whether or not creation took place in six days or was this simply a figure of speech? There are those who hold to the view that the earth is about six thousand years old, not billions of years in age, and that God created the heavens and the earth and all that they contain in a literal six-day event. My own belief is that God is powerful enough to have spoken creation into existence, creating all that is within six days, and giving it the appearance of having age. Adam was not created as an infant, but as a fully grown man, so why could God not have created the heavens and the earth with the same built-in look of the appearance of age? Others believe that this account was figurative and that creation took place over a longer period of time and that the six days were figurative speech or symbolic, and that the earth is billions of years old. I have listened to a creation scientist and an evolutionist debate the age of the earth using carbon dating, and with the same data, they came to different conclusions about the age of the earth. How can the same data lead to different conclusions? Obviously, they have different starting points and come with different pre-suppositions regarding their beliefs. There are those within the Christian community who hold to an evolutionary concept of creation (evolution within a species), believing that God created everything but through the evolutionary processes. Since none of us were there at the beginning, this debate will go on until the day we all die!

Since divorce rates among the Christian community are on a par with those outside of the church, the issue of divorce and remarriage is not only a crucial debate, it is ever present. I am one who has experienced divorce and remarriage, so not only is this issue personal, it is one I have struggled with greatly over the years.

Let me say upfront that the design for marriage is one of covenant and of permanence. It is to be reflective of the covenant we have with Christ, and as such is important in what it reflects about that covenant relationship. That being said, *Matthew 19:3–9* is quoted widely and often to support the view that divorce and remarriage is strictly forbidden except in cases of adultery, which then allows divorce to occur.

Having been through a divorce and remarriage that did not have this element involved (adultery) has given me cause to have much reflection on what the Bible has to say about divorce and remarriage and, as importantly, what is not addressed. For example, physical abuse is not addressed by Jesus or Paul. What does one tell someone who is being physically abused (in most cases, the husband is the perpetrator)? Do you tell them to just "hang in there" while getting abused and beaten? What about those who are emotionally and psychologically abused? This one is a bit tricky because such emotions do not carry with them the external scars that physical abuse carries. There are those who would say that (a) divorce is wrong in all cases and (b) once divorced, positions in the church (deacon, elder, overseer) are never to be considered for such a person.

The flip side of this coin is those churches which have no guidelines other than love and counsel for divorce at the drop of a hat! Either extreme creates a dilemma for the church. On the one hand, divorce is often treated as if it is the "unpardonable sin" and those who have experienced it as if they have leprosy. On the other, "no fault" divorce in our legal system has made it much too easy, and so divorce is treated as if it is a minor cold or just another day in the life, so move on!

Scripture is fairly clear that God hates divorce (Malachi 2:16), and that divorce other than for the cause of adultery is not looked upon favorably. That being said, people need a lot of grace and a lot of love and understanding from those in the church after a divorce has occurred. No one knows the full circumstances behind why a decision is made to carry through with divorce, so we should be cautious before making judgments in this regard. We don't always have all of the facts. Perhaps this is why it is so very important that marriage does not take place in a vacuum in the first place, and that wise counsel is sought before entering into marriage. Even a great marriage has its bumps-in-the-road and days of peril and trouble, so two people entering into this covenant should not do so with blinders on.

This will continue to be an issue in the church, and good people will not agree on how to handle someone who has been divorced and remarried. And we must realize that we should learn how to disagree agreeably before we cast one another into the pit!

Lastly, there are divergent views on how we are to understand the relationship of Israel and the church. One view holds that the church is the "new Israel" and is the continuation of the covenants made in the Old Testament, fulfilled in the New Testament through Jesus Christ. A second view makes a clear distinction between Israel and the Church and believes that Israel and the twelve tribes will be restored in the new heavens and the new earth. Yet another view holds that Israel and the Church are distinct, yet the same. And then there are those who question whether or not we are discussing the "chosen people" of the Old Testament (Israel) or the nation of Israel as it exists today (nationalistic Israel), and whether or not there is a distinction between the two or are they one and the same? Covenant theologians hold to one view, dispensational theologians hold to another, and historic pre-millenialists hold to another (though they are more closely aligned with dispensational thought). Sometimes, these disagreements have gotten, and do get, rather testy and nasty, and each believes that the hermeneutical approach that is taken by their own particular school of thought is the correct one.

Who is to say is correct? All schools of thought quote Scripture to support their views. I personally tend to lean toward the covenant view because of the promises made to Abraham are fulfilled in the person of Jesus Christ, and I have been "grafted in" and "adopted" as a child of God, not because I am Jewish, but because I have been granted grace through the mercy of God through the death and resurrection of Jesus Christ. The "veil of the temple was torn in two" (Luke 23:45, Matthew 27:51), signifying the separation between God and man had been restored, and we could enter the "holy of holies" because Jesus had paid the sacrifice for our sins.

Because I believe this, however, doesn't mean that I break fellowship with those who believe otherwise. My salvation, their salvation, is not dependent upon what we believe about Israel and the Church.

As I stated at the first of this chapter, getting in a huff about minutia does more harm than it does to bring us together. As long as we can agree that Jesus is Lord and that He died on the cross for our sins and was raised on the third day, then we can have fellowship together! Paul was clear that "if we have hoped in Christ in this life only, we are of all men most to be pitied" (1 Cor. 15:19), emphasizing that what we rally around is the core truth of Christ's death and resurrection, not the other negotiables that are important, but not crucial to our salvation and our joining together. Our "pet sounds" are these important truths!

CHAPTER 13

Caroline No

"Where did your long hair go? Where is the girl I used to know? How could you lose that happy glow? Oh, Caroline, No."

—Brian Wilson/Tony Asher

"If our lives do not reflect the fruit of following Jesus, then we are foolish to think that we are actually followers of Jesus in the first place."

—David Platt

"An old tradition sorts the difficulties we face in the life of faith into the categories of world, flesh, and devil... World is an atmosphere, a mood. It is nearly as hard for a sinner to recognize the world's temptations as it is for a fish to discover impurities in the water... We know that the spiritual atmosphere in which we live erodes faith, dissipates hope and corrupts love, but it is hard to put our fingers on what is wrong."

—Eugene Peterson

"No fact of contemporary Western life is more evident than its growing distrust of final truth and its implacable questioning of any sure word."
—Carl F. H. Henry

"The grass withers, the flower fades, but the word of our God will stand forever."
—Isaiah 40:8

If you have lived long enough, at times a wave of nostalgia will sweep over you and take you back to times when you think on good memories from earlier times, when you like to remember those times as if you were living in a dream world that was just almost perfect. With such remembering, we were always happier, always prettier and more handsome, always more athletic, always smarter, and seemed to live in this bubble of perfection. Or so it seems.

The sentiment expressed in the song for which this chapter is titled is one that longs for earlier times, yearns for happier times, that wonders what happened to this person I once knew. Such sentiment is not foreign to the ways in which each of us thinks about the past and longs for things to be so easy, so simple, so lacking with drama, so lacking with complexity. For those of us who were children in the 1950s and 1960s, life can be remembered as being fairly uncomplicated and carefree. The guys in their blue jeans and a little dab of Brylcreem in their hair, the girls with the bobby socks and loafers and hula skirts or yellow polka dot bikinis. And more likely than not, the teachers you had in school were also the same ones you had teaching Sunday school classes at your church. If you didn't attend church services, you at least knew about them and thought that maybe you should be there. It was the world of *Leave It to Beaver*, *Ozzie and Harriett*, *The Donna Reed Show*, *Tom and Jerry*, *Howdy Doody*, *Bozo the Clown*, *The Andy Griffith Show*, *Red Skelton*, *Gunsmoke*, *Bonanza*, and *The Ed Sullivan Show*. Even as I am writing this, flashbacks to some of those shows gives me a longing for that sense of loss that can accompany the thought that perhaps it was a time of near perfection.

When I wake up from that dream, however, I am brought to the realization that even in the midst of such dreaminess, there were things happening that would affect the flow of history even to this day. Certainly important events such as three assassinations, the elevation of the Vietnam War, the rise of the hippie movement, Woodstock, the civil rights movement, the rise of rock and roll, and the seemingly sudden challenge to the moral values that had been the status quo for decades made those years, as Dickens had penned a century earlier, "the best of times and the worst of times." As Buffalo Springfield would sing, "There's somethin' happenin' here. What it is ain't exactly clear."

In this book, I have attempted to explore and explain as much about Christian thought and living as the limitations of the song titles and my own limitations would allow me to do. As I was browsing through a couple of bookstores this past week, the thought occurred to me, why would anyone want to write another book? There are volumes upon volumes of books that fill our bookstores, our libraries, and now e-books that fill our computers. *What is one more book among the millions that have been written?* I thought

As I pondered this, I realized that I had wanted to write a book for some time that would explain some of the theological concepts in simple terms. Beyond that, I also wanted to make it clear that as followers of Christ, those of us who claim the label "Christian" must live what we say we believe and must, as David Platt has challenged us to do so clearly in his own books and ministry, take up our crosses daily and follow Jesus. In doing so, we may have the opportunity to see real revival, real awakening in our time. But to do so, we must understand better where we find ourselves and see very clearly that we are not living in the '50s or '60s, and that there is "somethin' happenin' here."

WHERE DID YOUR LONG HAIR GO?

Western culture, so profoundly influenced for centuries by both the Reformation and the Enlightenment periods, has taken such a dramatic shift that if you were to take someone like my dad, who died in 1973, and drop him into our current cultural malaise, he would not recognize where he was and would be shocked by this shift. Other than the enormous technological changes and advances that have occurred (such as this computer I am typing on and the iPhone I use exclusively for my telephone), the overwhelming changes that dominate our moral and ethical landscape would be astounding.

Statistical studies show that more and more young couples are living together rather than marrying. It has become rather common to become pregnant and have babies outside of wedlock, and rather than weep over this development, our culture applauds and extols them and puts them on the covers of our tabloid magazines. Our television shows are dominated by situations such as this, and no show is complete anymore without at least one homosexual or lesbian couple as part of the plot. Scenes that were once considered taboo for the small screen are now so common that we, as a culture, have grown so accustomed to seeing what amounts to soft porn that we no longer even flinch when it comes on. As mentioned earlier, movies have become so verbally and physically graphic that even grandchildren think nothing of the violence and sexual overtones that fill the large screen because that is what the "new normal" is for them. A very long way from Clark Gable in *Gone with the Wind*.

Not surprisingly, along with this we have seen a rather dramatic change in the number of young people who no longer claim any religious affiliation. According to the Pew Research Center, "Between 2007 and 2014, the Christian share of the population fell from 78.4% to 70.6%. While the drop is *particularly pronounced* among young adults, it is occurring among Americans of all ages." Part of the drop may be explained by the possibility that people are being more honest with their answers and no longer feel the need to say that they are "Christian" when they know they are not. Nonetheless, the drop in a seven-year period is not only dramatic; it is reflective of where we find ourselves as a culture that is no longer as strongly influenced by Judeo-Christian values.

What explains this? Where, in a manner of speaking, did our long hair go? What has happened in Western culture (and this would include most of Europe, which has been in spiritual decline for longer than America) that we no longer find it necessary to believe in God, to believe in values, to believe in morals? How can our cultural decline be explained?

How Could You Lose That Happy Glow?

Ultimately, we have the clash of two mindsets, two world views that are diametrically opposed to each other. One says that "the cosmos is all there is" and places man at the center of the universe. This view holds to a non-supernatural belief, and that we were created out of a collision of atoms that somehow eventually formed humans and gave us the human race as we are today, albeit through a long process of evolution. The second view says that there is a personal, triune God who created the universe and all that it contains "ex nihilo" or out of nothing, and is intimately involved with His creation. Obviously, this view holds to a supernatural belief and places God at the center of the universe around which everything else revolves.

But how do we see these views played out on the stage of human drama? Over time, I have given this a great deal of thought and have broken this down into four different areas of influence: sociological, political, philosophical, and spiritual.

Sociological. Among many of the areas where we could begin, I begin with the most basic of influences, and that is the breakdown of the home and family. It is from our homes and our families where so much of how we see the world and respond to the world has its roots. I don't need to quote statistics to point out what has happened within our family structures that has changed and influenced our culture. Within the black community, for example, it has been pointed out time and time again how many fathers are absentee when it comes to being around for their children and how detrimental this has been within that community and for society. Lest we think, however, that it has been only in the black community, let us not try to fool ourselves into believing that the white community is immune. Quite the contrary.

Divorce and absenteeism has risen over the past sixty years, which is my exact lifetime. I, myself, have experienced divorce and worked very hard to maintain my responsibilities to my own children, but I have also observed many fathers who abandon their responsibilities to their children whenever a divorce is involved. This has had a very negative impact on their children and on society as a whole and is one factor in the decline of the family.

Public education, especially in our colleges, has been a major influence in how young people perceive reality and the views that have been adopted. Under the guise of a so-called broadminded education, what has actually been occurring has been an indoctrination to views that question the validity of biblical and absolute truth. Comedian Jerry Seinfeld recently mentioned that he would stay away from college campuses because they were the bastions of "PC" (Political Correctness). My own experience in college, at a very conservative public institution in the 1970s, was an eye-opener when encountering those who preached "being open-minded" but were anything, but this if you disagreed with their liberal and anti-Christian views. In fact, I found these people to be the most closed minded individuals of any that I encountered. As it is today, there was no dialogue, only a continual drivel driven monologue.

In public schools, discipline has all but essentially been removed so that teacher's hands are tied when needing to bring such discipline to the classroom. My wife is a former school teacher, and the challenges she faced in the classroom because of this were enormous. And rather than teaching basic things such as reading, writing, and arithmetic so that our youth will have a solid foundation for the future, our schools are now strapped with having to "teach the test." In other words, prepare students to learn how to pass the mandatory state tests rather than teaching them actual thought processes and learning skills.

The response to this has been a rise in private schools and home schooling. The upside of this has been that those who can afford private schools or who actually do home school have seen a vast improvement in the learning skills and abilities of their children. The downside has been to take the influence of Christian families out of the public sector in education. How, one may ask, are we to be "salt and light," if we completely remove ourselves out of contact with public education? On the other hand, how can we justify not doing this to improve the education, discipline, and moral character development that our children and youth receive? It is a difficult balance to achieve.

Another such influence has been the disproportional influence of "Hollywood" on our social mores. We are constantly bombarded on the small screen and on the big screen with messages that challenge Christian truth. *Romans 12:1–2* reminds us that we are to be "transformed by the renewing of our minds," and what we fill our minds with will eventually spill forth in how we live. Unfortunately, the influence of Hollywood tends to fill our minds with those ideas and images that are detrimental to the Christian faith, with few exceptions. Another part of this influence is the manner in which we soak up the social, political, and spiritual views espoused by actors and actresses as if they know something more than we do because they seem to be bigger than life due to our culture's infatuation with celebrity. As Isaiah said so clearly, "Come, let us reason together!" These actors and actresses are just people like the rest of us, desperately in need of redemption as are we all.

I would add that the 24-7 continuity of media "news coverage" contributes to the dumbing down and spiritual apathy that we find ourselves facing. News, by its very nature, tends to present primarily negative stories because that is what sells. The more sensational, the better it sells, and what is sensational about people doing positive and good deeds? So we are bombarded all day and all night (if we so wish) with cable news and broadcast news and network news that brings us the news, without us noticing that such news is edited by those who control those airwaves and satellites and cable lines. We never get the full story, the full truth, but an edited version of what others who create this news perceive as "the truth" and who present this "truth" as the whole enchilada, the whole story, the true, factual data. Except, we only hear and see what they report and what the camera, in its limited scope, is able to show us. More relativity at work.

Finally, one other such sociological influence that tends to move us toward a moral and spiritual decay is the marketing schemes of Madison Avenue. Sex sells, so everything from toothpaste to automobiles is advertised with this in mind. Want to be sexier? Buy this toothpaste. Want to feel sexier? Drive this car. Half-naked women are used to advertise just about any product, and one has to wonder, at the end of the commercial, just what was the product they were selling? Cameras, bug spray, toothpicks, pens, staples, paper products, books, beer, and on and on become your path to a sexier you. And one must be hip, cool, and keeping up with the Jones (or in our modern society, the Kardashians) in order to make it in our culture. Oddly enough, when buying any of these products, I have yet to feel or think that I am sexier because I now own the product.

Sexier because I bought a certain brand of bug spray? I just want dead wasps! Yet the marketing used for just about any product is designed to draw us in, whether the advertising is actually true or not. Truth is not the issue; selling is the issue. And we get sold on the idea that more and more is better and better. Consumption is both the engine that drives our culture and the bane of our existence. A rather sharp two-edged sword.

In his magnificent book *A Long Obedience in the Same Direction*, Eugene Peterson provides an excellent summary to this section. He writes:

> Rescue me from the lies of advertisers who claim to know what I need and what I desire, from the lies of entertainers who promise a cheap way of joy, from the lies of politicians who pretend to instruct me in power and morality, from the lies of psychologists who offer to shape my behavior and my morals so that I will live long, happily and successfully, from the lies of religionists who "heal the wounds of this people lightly," from the lies of moralists who pretend to promote me to the office of captain of my fate, from the lies of pastors who "get rid of God's command so you won't be inconvenienced in following the religious fashions!" (Peterson, *A Long Obedience in the Same Direction*, pg.27)

Philosophical. In another chapter, I mentioned the importance of world views and how we each live by some world view, whether we recognize it or not. Of all of the philosophies competing for viability and credibility, one particular philosophy dominates our culture above all others. Pragmatism is by far the dominant view that permeates our culture.

Other philosophies certainly have their own influence. Existentialism has played a part in influencing society, through the writings of Albert Camus and Jean Paul Sartre in particular. At its core, this philosophy says one's existence is validated by simply doing something rather than nothing. Thus, one may walk an old lady across the street or push her in front of a bus. Either way, you have validated your existence, but right or wrong is not the issue. Nihilism follows on the heels of this philosophy and ultimately leads to despair. Nothing is meaningful, life itself is meaningless. We die and become food for worms, so eat, drink, and be merry for tomorrow, your meaningless existence may end.

However, American culture in particular is driven by pragmatism, for the basic teaching of pragmatism is that "truth is whatever works." When I was taking a course in college on pragmatism, I distinctly remember thinking what an "air tight" philosophy this seems to be. The illustration often used to foster the idea of pragmatism is that of an elephant and a blind man. If a blind man touches the trunk of an elephant, how does he describe the elephant? If he touches the leg of an elephant, how does he then describe the elephant? If he touches the tail or the body of said elephant, how is this elephant then described? Truth, we are told, is the same way. It is all relative, and like beauty, such truth lies in the eye or feel or thought of the beholder. Thus, all religions become the same and all paths to God are equally valid because, like the blind man and the elephant, any way the elephant is described is true. Truth is or becomes whatever works for you.

As I pointed out in the class, the problem with this is that we are not blind. We do not blindly choose what truth is or what is falsehood but have been given both reasoning powers and clear direction on what the options available to us mean and what are their consequences. And no one lives consistently with the view that there are no absolutes.

The professor of this class, who was quite brilliant, and I were walking down the sidewalk together one day after class, and he mentioned that he did not believe in absolutes. I mentioned that I did. Interestingly enough, a week or so later, a letter to the editor showed up in our school newspaper from this professor complaining about another ham radio operator who was interfering with his own signal and how wrong this was for this other operator to infringe on his frequency. I asked him how, if he did not believe in absolutes, could this other operator be wrong if no such category existed for the professor? No one lives consistently with the pragmatic view because at some point, the premise that "truth is what works" gets challenged. This view only works until someone gets into our space and infringes on what we perceive to be the truth. We discover rather quickly that all "truths" are not valid in such a world.

We see this view dominate our marketing. Advertising must be true because it works! Even when such advertising borders on out right falseness, we still buy into whatever is being advertised. How do we know? Because we are a consumer driven society, and the philosophy doing the driving is pragmatism.

In the world of religion, this view was and is still influenced by William James and his seminal work entitled "The Varieties of Religious Experience." Written as more of a psychological work, it pointed out the value of all religious experience as being equally valid. Again, truth is whatever works. As I mentioned earlier, the pastor who said he believed in Christianity where he pastored because "it worked." Not, mind you, it is truth because it is the truth but because it worked. Such a mindset underscores the influence of the philosophy of pragmatism. And such an influence also underscores at least some of the reason we have a culture that has turned from its Judeo Christian heritage to a culture of relativity in matters of truth.

Political. I would be amiss to avoid or not mention the influence of the political world on where we find ourselves today. In many ways, it is ultimately a spiritual issue, but politics and the political world have a powerful influence on our culture.

As Christians, we are commanded to submit to and pray for our governmental leaders, even when we may not agree with their policies and/or agenda.(Romans 13:1–6, 1 Peter 2:13–17, 1 Timothy 2:1–3). Of course, there are justifiable times of civil disobedience (such as when Peter would not stop from preaching about Jesus). If we look at some of the statements made by the Founding Fathers and some of those who followed (most notably, Abraham Lincoln), it would be difficult to agree with some of the revisionist historians who want to rewrite history and attribute our beginnings to something other than a very strong Christian influence. Certainly there were deists (for example, Thomas Jefferson), agnostics (Benjamin Franklin), and those who were not Christians, but the primary influence in the beginnings of this country was Judeo-Christian values and thought. We were not nor ever have been a theocracy or even a "Christian" nation, but we were founded upon Christian principles that came out of the influence of the Reformation and the Word of God. Even philosophers such as Thomas Paine, who in turn influenced the authors of the Constitution, were themselves influenced by Judeo-Christian principles. As my pastor said recently, "America was founded as a haven for people seeking liberty to practice their faith without persecution."

That being said, where do we find ourselves today? Even with all of the awesome technological advances that have been made in the last fifty years, the moral decline has been alarming. We are still reeling from the effects of that blight in our history which allowed slavery and defined black individuals as "3/5 of a person." (Technically, what was actually done as a compromise was to count every five "negroes" as three people, and this was done as a compromise so that the South did not have more representatives than other Northern states and so that taxation would not hit the Southern states so hard.) And the humanistic world view that our culture has adopted has put us in the middle of an immoral storm that seems to have no end.

Politically, the response that we had to the Great Depression in the form of the "New Deal" brought some changes that were necessary but opened the door very widely to our current entitlement mentality. I quote something our pastor wrote recently in an article.

"Alexander Fraser Tytler (1748–1813), a Scottish professor at the University of Edinburgh, wrote the following in *The Decline and Fall of the Athenian Republic:* 'A democracy cannot exist as permanent form of government. It can only exist until the voters discover that they can vote themselves money from the Public Treasury. From that moment on the majority always votes for the candidates promising the most benefits from the Public Treasury with a result that *democracy always collapses over loose fiscal policy.* The average age of the world's greatest civilizations has been 200 years. These nations have progressed through the following sequence:

(1) From bondage to spiritual faith
(2) From spiritual faith to great courage
(3) From great courage to liberty
(4) From liberty to abundance
(5) From abundance to selfishness
(6) From selfishness to complacency
(7) From complacency to apathy
(8) From apathy to dependency
(9) From dependency to bondage."

We are at a time in our history in which we, as a culture, have come to think that government and politicians have all the answers. And we have discovered that we can vote ourselves money out of the

Public Treasury. Nothing akin to government and politicians having all the answers could be further from the truth, and it is dangerous to believe this to be so, for the only true change that ever lasts is a change of the heart, and the only person who can bring about that change is Jesus Christ. Yes, we need laws to keep order, and we need government for those things that a government is supposed to provide, such as order, protection, and life and liberty. But the only change that moves a culture in a moral and ethical direction that provides for true freedom is the change that God brings in a person when that person is truly "born again." And we are desperately in need of a real awakening, a real revival. Only in such a move of God do the politics of government take on an entirely different direction.

Spiritual. Paul writes in *Ephesians 6:12*, "For our struggle is not against flesh and blood, but against the rulers, against the powers against the world forces of this darkness, against the spiritual forces of wickedness in the heavenly places." He also writes in *2 Corinthians 10:3–4*, "For though we walk in the flesh, we do not war according to the flesh, for the weapons of our warfare are not of the flesh, but divinely powerful for the destruction of fortresses." He speaks further to the spiritual battle that goes on in the world when he says in 2 Corinthians 4:3–4, "And even if our gospel is veiled, it is veiled to those who are perishing, in whose case the god of this world has blinded the minds of the unbelieving, that they might not see the light of the gospel of the glory of Christ, who is the image of God."

I believe that much of what we are experiencing in Western culture has more to do with the spiritual battles taking place in the heavenlies than any other one factor. While sociological, philosophical, and political changes are certainly factors, Paul reminds us several times that the real battle takes place in unseen places. And as we draw closer to the end-times (and every day draws us closer, just by the nature of another day passing), such activity seems to be increasing in both volume and intensity.

Almost all of our long held and strongly held Christian beliefs are under attack and under scrutiny. Marriage and family as an institution, with one man-one woman as the standard, is under more attack than I ever thought would be possible. Being politically correct is more important than doing what is right in the eyes of the Lord. The nature of man and our propensity toward sin seems to be approaching the days of Sodom and Gomorrah, for we seem to have little or no remorse about the wrong and evil things we do. And the world looks at our own addiction to materialism and wonders why they should hear a message that doesn't appear to look any different from what they already believe. Such hypocrisy flies in the face of the true gospel message.

How can the world not scoff when it sees things such as a ministry that is raising $65 million dollars so that this ministry can buy a G650 Gulf Stream Jet so that the pastor can fly around in comfort to "lead the flock"? This is just one example of extreme measures in ministries that feed on the sheep, that feed on the poor, that feed on the gullible, and misplaced trust through slick marketing, that preach a false gospel of "health, wealth, and prosperity." Did not Paul warn of just such things as spiritual matters heated up? *First Timothy 4:1–2 says,* "The Spirit explicitly says that in later times some will fall away from the faith, paying attention to deceitful spirits and doctrines of demons." 2 Timothy 3:1-4 says, "But realize this, that in the last days difficult times will come. For men will be lovers of self, lovers of money, boastful, arrogant, revilers, disobedient to parents, ungrateful, unholy, unloving, irreconcilable, malicious gossips, without self-control, brutal, haters of good, treacherous, reckless, conceited, *lovers of pleasure rather than lovers of God.*" Peter writes in *2 Peter 3:3,* "Know this first of all, that in the last days mockers will come with their mocking, following after their own lusts, and saying, 'Where is the promise of His coming?'"

The spiritual battle taking place has always taken place, from the first temptation in the Garden of Eden to our current times and civilizations. Such battles are nothing new. Look at any period in history and you will find hypocrisy and corruption in the church and in society. And each generation has thought that their generation epitomized what the Bible had to say about end-times and believed that they, indeed, were living in those times. Who among us knows? Certainly, many have tried to predict and have obviously failed in those predictions. Rightly so. Even Jesus said that "no man knows the day or hour." But we can see that our world is vastly different than it was fifty years ago in how our basis for values has changed and how, overall, such change has created the moral and spiritual vacuum we are experiencing. And it is what we cannot see that is as important as anything we can see, for the spiritual battles taking place in the unseen world have enormous influence on what happens in the known and seen world.

CAN WE EVER BRING IT BACK ONCE THEY HAVE GONE?

The short answer to this question is yes. An emphatic and resounding yes. But there are some requirements in order for this answer to stand.

First, we who believe we are Christian and who claim the name "Christian" need to make certain that we actually are what we say. As David Platt says, "People who claim to be Christian while their lives look no different from the rest of the world are clearly not Christians" (David Platt, *Follow Me*, pg. 18). He goes on to say the following. "Spiritual deception is dangerous—and damning. Any one of us can fool ourselves… The Bible says that the god of this world (Satan) is blinding the minds of unbelievers to keep them from knowing Christ. Couldn't it be that one of the ways the devil is doing this is by deceiving people into believing they are Christians when they are not?" (Platt, pg. 18).

I once preached a sermon I entitled "The First Word of the Gospel." That word is *repent*. It is the first word John the Baptist spoke to those hearing him, it is the first word Jesus spoke as He began His ministry, and it was the first thing Peter said when asked, "What should we do?" After preaching this, I had a deacon in the church challenge me and say that the first word or thing we are told to do is to "believe on the Lord Jesus and thou shall be saved." I pointed out that the demons believe and shudder, but they are certainly not saved. Believing without repenting is simply making a mental ascent without having to change and move in the opposite direction, which is what repentance will produce and what repent actually means. Again, Platt writes, "Almost unknowingly, we all have a tendency to redefine Christianity according to our own tastes, preferences, church traditions, and cultural norms. Slowly, subtly, we take the Jesus of the Bible and twist him into someone with whom we are a little more comfortable… In the end, we create a nice, non-offensive, politically correct, middle-class, American Jesus who looks just like us and thinks just like us" (Platt, pg. 76).

In order for a change in direction in our culture to occur, we need to begin by making sure our own house is in order, and that repentance is at the very core of who we claim to be as Christians.

Second, we must pray that we become hungry for the word of God. Those who call themselves evangelical, whether they are Baptists, Presbyterian, Bible church, etc. claim to be people "of the Word." The problem is that we don't really know the Word, and it is why we can be so easily deceived.

I am saying this, in part, because I confess that I went through a long period in my own life in which my hunger for the Word of God went on a "hunger strike." I read the word very little and certainly did not study it as I should have been doing. It was dead to me, and

I just sort of went through the motions and that very little. It is why I say we must *pray* that we become hungry for God's Word because we cannot muster up enough hunger on our own to desire the food that lies within His Word. And it is that food that gives us life! So we need to desperately pray to become deeply hungry for God's word so that it changes the way we think and thus changes who we are and how we live. This will, in turn, help to bring a change to our world.

Third, we must pray that God breaks us of our comfortable, apathetic faith. Like most of us, I have grown up and spent most of my Christian life in a very comfortable place. I like my comfort. I like comfortable pews, I like being comfortably entertained in church, I like the comfort of coming and going to worship when I choose and when I please, and I like the comfort of a me-centered gospel. Who among us doesn't like to be comfortable? But when I read the words and commands of Jesus, it challenges my comfort and that makes me uncomfortable.

We worry about ISIS, we worry about having enough money, we worry about having enough stuff, we worry about our politics and our government, we worry about our children, and we worry about the future. But our biggest challenge, our greatest threat is our own apathy in our faith. It is not all of these external forces that pose the greatest threat. It is being or becoming the lukewarm believer, the lukewarm church that poses the greatest threat to our future. So we must pray that we become "hot" again if we are to see change and revival come to our culture.

Finally, you and I must take what we often quote and hear quoted from 2 Chronicles 7:14 to heart: "And My people who are called by My name humble themselves and pray, and seek My face and turn from their wicked ways, then I will hear from heaven, will forgive their sin, and will heal their land." God is, of course, speaking to Solomon about the children of Israel and is not, contrary to what many seem to believe, making this promise to America. But He is making the promise to "people who are called by My name," and that would be all Christians at this point. The central focus of this is prayer and repentance. God's healing of "their land" was dependent upon His people actually praying and "turning from their wicked ways," which is what we have seen is what repentance is supposed to be. This is a passage that we often hear to admonish us, but we all need to adhere to what this passage is saying. I am chief among those needing to follow this call.

In our culture's history, we have experienced times of "awakening." In Jonathan Edwards's time in the early to middle eighteenth century, he was involved in two periods we have come to know as the Great Awakening. There were times of awakening in the mid-1800s and early in the twentieth century. The closest we have seen in our lifetimes to any sort of "awakening" was the Jesus Movement that began in the late 1960s and carried over into the 1970s and '80s. We are in deep need of a true, nationwide, worldwide "awakening." We find ourselves, as a culture, somewhere in between the period of apathy and dependency that I mentioned earlier. Only a powerful move of God will shake us from this place, and only God has the power to bring about such a movement. While we are certainly involved in such a movement, and prayer and repentance are needed, only God can bring about such a revival, such an awakening. We cannot force His hand, we cannot do slick marketing to promote such a plan, we cannot get another committee together to vote on such a plan, we cannot budget our finances for such a plan; what we can do is pray.

Can we, as the song says, ever bring it back once it is gone? Unlike the answer given in the song ("Caroline No"), *yes* we can, but only in God's way and in God's timing. Let us pray for that and be prepared for when it comes. *Wouldn't it be nice? Oh, Caroline, yes!*

ADDENDUM

SYSTEMATIC THEOLOGY

Most people in our churches know little about what is known as "systematic theology." It is taught in seminaries, primarily, and is rarely mentioned within the confines of the church walls. Often, it is met with a certain amount of skepticism and is not considered to be important except for preachers and theologians.

This addendum is not going to make the skepticism disappear, but it is important to have some familiarity with systematic theology and its contribution to the life of the church.

Biblical doctrine can be codified or systematized in different ways. Different theologians and schools of thought have certainly done this when it has come to organizing doctrinal beliefs and theology.

So what is systematic theology? In very simple terms, systematic theology is a way of organizing biblical doctrines, developed throughout church history, as a means of defining, codifying, and clarifying those doctrines in a system or a systematic manner.

What I am attempting to do with this addendum is to give a basic synopsis of those doctrines and the ways in which they are systematized. There are many who have written books on systematic theology, but I will focus on three I am familiar with and which have been used often as a basis for studying systematic theology. Those three are William G. T. Shedd and his three-volume "Dogmatic Theology," Charles Hodge and his three-volume "Systematic

Theology," and Lewis Sperry Chafer and his four or eight-volume "Systematic Theology." Others, such as A. H. Strong, have also written and taught systematic theology, but we are not going to cover everyone.

As I do this, let me say I am drawing upon these resources for this addendum and not going specifically through each one. I am providing this information just because I think it is good to know and, at least, have some familiarity with theology in this manner.

Generally speaking, systematic theology can be broken down into the following categories:

1. Bibliology and Prolegomena – The Bible
2. Theology Proper – the study of God
3. Christology – the study of Jesus Christ
4. Pneumatology – the Holy Spirit
5. Angelology – the study of angels
6. Anthropology – the study of man
7. Soteriology – the study of salvation
8. Ecclesiology – the study of the Church
9. Eschatology – Prophecy and the end times.

BIBLIOLOGY AND PROLEGOMENA

This deals with the Bible and how the Bible came to be the Bible. This area of doctrinal study looks at things such as how we came to have the canon of scripture, what were the guidelines for determining what was to be considered God's Word and what was not, the biblical parchments, the historical settings for the development of scripture, and the doctrine of inspiration and authority of the Bible.

THEOLOGY PROPER

Basically, this is the study of God and His nature and attributes. It can also entail a look at philosophical arguments for the existence of God and the study of the triune God or God in three persons. It may also look at those views which are antitheistic and present arguments opposed to the theistic view of a triune God.

CHRISTOLOGY

The study of the person and work of Jesus Christ. It looks at both his divine and human natures, and how they coexist. This area of study will also look at the place Jesus holds in the Trinity as the Son and what that role entails, especially as it relates to salvation.

PNEUMATOLOGY

This is the study of the person and work of the Holy Spirit. What His role involves, His place in the Trinity, and the roles He plays in the life of a believer and in the church. It may also touch on the "gifts" of the Spirit and what those gifts involve as it relates to the role of the Holy Spirit.

ANGELOLOGY

As the name would indicate, this is the study of angels. It looks at both the role of angels and those angels who have fallen and are considered followers of Lucifer or Satan. As such, the study will also get into demonology.

ANTHROPOLOGY

The Greek root of this word "Anthropos" is the word for *man,* so the study involves looking at the origin of man, in both body and spirit. It will entail looking at different theories of man's origin and development and the fall of man and its consequences, especially as it relates to sin and man's basic nature. The study will also consider the provision made for man as it relates to sin.

SOTERIOLOGY

This is the study of salvation and just what is and was involved in salvation. It will consider such things as who the Savior is, why a Savior was and is necessary, the sufferings of Christ, and what was accomplished by the sufferings and subsequent death and atonement of Christ. This study may also consider areas such as the doctrine of election, justification, sanctification, and glorification. It may also look at different views of how this salvation is and has been viewed historically.

ECCLESIOLOGY

The study of Ecclesiology is the study of the church. This study considers it biblically, historically, doctrinally, and practically. In some studies, the distinction between Israel and the church is considered, and how and if they are one and the same or a continuance or completely separate from one another. The bride and bridegroom theme is one that may be considered, and the structure and governing of the church is also considered.

ESCHATOLOGY

As was mentioned in chapter 5 of the book, eschatology is the study of prophecy and last things in Scripture. It is the study of what is considered to be what the future holds for the world and the church. It also considers past fulfillments of prophecy as found in both the Old and New Testaments and the doctrines of heaven and hell. There may also be included in this study the role of Israel and what, if any, significance Israel plays in the return of Christ. This study will, obviously, consider the teachings on the Second Coming of Christ and those things possibly leading up to the Second Coming.

If one were to embark upon a rather serious and deeper study of Christianity and its doctrines, at some point along the way, that person will go much deeper into the study of systematic theology. I have provided only a very limited and brief synopsis, which I hope proves helpful. The definitions and descriptions I have given are my own personal understandings of systematic theology and what it may encompass. There are better definitions that exist, I am sure. I have simply wanted to present these in terms that are simplified and understandable. And, honestly, they go about as deep as I can go!

BIBLIOGRAPHY

Bettenson, Henry. *Doctrines of the Christian Church.* London, Oxford: New York: Oxford University. Bloesch, Donald, *Crumbling Foundations.* Grand Rapids: Zondervan Publishing House, 1984, Press, 1980.

Bloesch, Donald. *Essential of Evangelical Theology,* 2 Volumes. Peabody, Ma.: Prince Press, 2001.

Bloesch, Donald. *Faith & Its Counterfeits.* Downers Grove, Il.: Inter-Varsity, Press, 1981.

Bloom, Alan. *The Closing of the American Mind.* New York: Simon and Schuster, 1987

Carlin, Peter Ames. *Catch A Wave: The Rise, Fall, and Redemption of the Beach Boys' Brian Wilson.* Rodale Publisher, 2006.

Colson, Charles. *How Now Shall We Live?* Wheaton, Il.: Tyndale House Publishers, 1999.

Colson, Charles. *Loving God.* Grand Rapids, Mi.: Zondervan Publishing House, 1983.

Edwards, Jonathan. *On Knowing Christ.* Carlisle, Pa.: Banner of Truth, 1990

Edwards, Jonathan. *The Religious Affections.* Carlisle, Pa.: Banner of Truth, 2001.

Fischer, John. *Making Real What I Already Believe.* Minneapolis: Bethany House Publishers, 1991.

Friesen, Gary. *Decision Making and the Will of God.* Sisters, Or.: Multnomah Publishers, 1980, 2004.

Geisler, Norman and Nix, William E. *A General Introduction to the Bible.* Chicago: Moody Press, 1979.

Gini, Al. *The Importance of Being Lazy.* New York: Routledge, 2003.

Granata, Charles L. *Wouldn't It Be Nice: Brian Wilson and the Making of Pet Sounds.* Chicago: A Capella Books, 2003.

Guinness, Os. *The American Hour.* New York: The Free Press, 1993.

Guinness, Os and Seel, John, editors. *No God But God.* Chicago: Moody Press 1992.

Henry, Carl F. H. *God, Revelation, and Authority, Vol. 1.* Waco, Word Books, 1976.

Hunter, James Davison. *Culture Wars.* New York: Harper-Collins, 1991.

Jacobs, Alan. *Original Sin: A Cultural History.* New York: Harper-Collins, 2008.

James, William. *Pragmatism.* Amherst, N.Y.: Prometheus Books, 1991.

Keller, Timothy. *The Reason for God.* New York: Riverhead Books, 2008.

Kelly, J. N. D. *Early Christian Doctrines.* San Francisco: Harper & Row, 1978.

Kierkegaard, Soren. *Provocations: Spiritual Writings of Kierkegaard* (edited by Moore, Charles) Farmington, Pa.: The Plough Publishing House, 1999.

Kyle, Richard. *The Last Days Are Here Again: A History of the End Times.* Grand Rapids: Baker Books, 1998.

Lake, Kyle. *Understanding God's Will.* Lake Mary, Fl.: Relevant Books, 2005.

Lasch, Christopher. *The Culture of Narcissism: American Life in an Age of Diminishing Expectations.* New York: W.W. Norton and Company, Inc., 1979.

Leaf, David. *The Beach Boys and the California Myth.* Philadelphia: Courage Books, 1978, 1985.

Miller, Donald. *Blue Like Jazz.* Nashville: Thomas Nelson, Inc. 2003.

Murray, Iain. *Jonathan Edwards: A New Biography.* Carlisle, Pa.: Banner of Truth, 1987.

Olasky, Marvin. *The Tragedy of American Compassion.* Washington, D.C.: Regnery Publishing, 1992.

Ortberg, John. *Everybody's Normal 'Til You Get To Know Them.* Grand Rapids: Zondervan Publishing, 2003.

Owen, John. *Sin and Temptation (compilation of essays from 1850–1853).* Portland, Or.: Multnomah Press, 1983.

Packer, J. I. *Knowing God.* Downers Grove, Il.: Inter-Varsity Press, 1977.

Peterson, Eugene. *A Long Obedience in the Same Direction.* Downers Grove, Il. Inter-Varsity Press, 1980, 2000.

Peterson, Jesse. *Scam: How The Black Leadership Exploits Black America.* Nashville: WND Books, 2003.

Pippert, Rebecca. *Hope Has Its Reasons.* Downers Grove, Il.: Inter-Varsity Press, 1989, 2001.

Plantinga, Cornelius Jr. *Not The Way It's Supposed To Be: A Breviary of Sin.* Grand Rapids: Wm. B. Eerdmans Publishing, 1996.

Riddlebarger, Kim. *A Case for Amillennialism: Understanding the End Times.* Grand Rapids; Leicester, England: Baker Books, Inter-Varsity Press.

Russell, Bertrand. *Why I Am Not a Christian.* New York: Simon and Schuster, 1957 (15th printing)

Sartre, Jean-Paul. *Existentialism and Human Emotions.* New York: Citadel Press, 1957 (Philosophical Library, Inc. copyright).

Schaeffer, Francis. *Genesis in Space and Time.* Downers Grove, Il.: Inter-Varsity Press, 1972, 1977.

Schaeffer, Francis. *The God Who Is There.* Downers Grove: Inter-Varsity Press, 1968, 1973.

Schaeffer, Francis. *No Little People, No Little Places.* Downers Grove: Inter-Varsity Press, 1974, 1975.

Schaeffer, Francis. *True Spirituality.* Wheaton, Il.: Tyndale House Publishers, 1971, 1976.

Schaeffer, Francis and Koop, C. Everett. *Whatever Happened to the Human Race?* Old Tappan, N.J.: Fleming H. Revell Co., 1979.

Sire, James. *The Universe Next Door: A World View Catalog.* Downers Grove: Inter-Varsity Press, 1976, 1997 (Third edition).

Sproul, R. C. *The Holiness of God.* Wheaton, Il.: Tyndale House Publishers, Inc., 1985, 1998.

Sterrett, T. Norton. *How to Understand Your Bible.* Downers Grove: Inter-Varsity Press, 1974.

Yancey, Philip. *Prayer: Does It Matter?* Grand Rapids: Zondervan, 2006.

Yancey, Philip. *What's So Amazing About Grace?* Grand Rapids: Zondervan, 1997.

Yancey, Philip. *The Jesus I Never Knew.* Grand Rapids: Zondervan, 1995.

Zacharias, Ravi. *Deliver Us From Evil: Restoring the Soul in a Disintegrating Culture.* Nashville: Word Publishing, 1997.

Zacharias, Ravi. *Jesus Among Other Gods.* Nashville: Word Publishing, 2000.

ABOUT THE AUTHOR

A graduate of Texas A&M University (B.A.) and Southwestern Baptist Theological Seminary (M.Div.), the author has a diverse background, which is one way of saying that he is still growing up and developing! Blessed by his wife of eighteen years, Kay, four grown children (two daughters and two stepchildren), and four grandchildren, he has a rich sense of humor and brings that into his communications, whether written or spoken. He continues to enjoy learning and enjoys most sports, having played baseball, basketball, and tennis, and continuing to enjoy golf. As a former trombone player and piano novice, his enjoyment of music extends from classical to swing to jazz to classic pop and rock to old hymns, and he has always enjoyed harmonic music, thus his passion for Brian Wilson and Beach Boys music. He currently lives in Tyler, Texas, with his wife and three dogs and the token cat. He has another book of poetry and essays (unpublished) and is currently writing a book on Christian sanctification. He is also preparing to write his first novel. His deepest desire is to live and communicate Christian truth in a way that is practical and real. This is his first published book.

CPSIA information can be obtained
at www.ICGtesting.com
Printed in the USA
FSOW02n0531240916
25325FS